The C. S. Lewis Centre is an international network of Christians from many different churches and traditions. Despite their differences, they are united by their commitment to historic Christianity.

There are a number of ways in which we work to achieve our aims. These include:

Dialogue

The Centre is a meeting point for Christians who would never normally talk to one another. We make it possible for people from a rich diversity of Christian traditions to engage in open, frank debate.

Education

The Centre bridges the gap between the college and the pew by providing top-quality education for Christians in their local churches. This is done through seminars, workshops, and conferences.

Research

We carry out research into the relationship between Christianity and the modern world. We seek to develop a distinctively Christian voice in response to the critical issues of the day.

Publishing

The Centre generates a variety of publications, including the C. S. Lewis Centre books being published, video and audio tapes, and occasional papers. We also produce a quarterly journal entitled *Leading Light.*

For further information, write to: The C. S. Lewis Centre, %Dr. Andrew Walker, Centre for Educational Studies, King's College London, Cornwall House Annex, Waterloo Road, London SE1 8TX. In the United States you can contact us by writing: The C.S. Lewis Centre, %Jeff Miller, Texas Wesleyan University, 1201 Wesleyan, Fort Worth, TX 76105-1536.

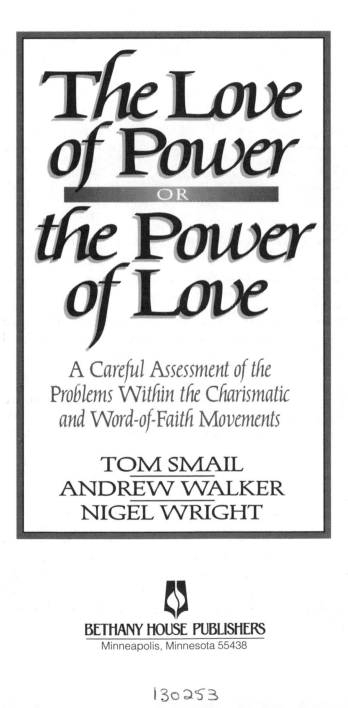

The Love of Power

OR

the Power of Love

A Careful Assessment of the
Problems Within the Charismatic
and Word-of-Faith Movements

TOM SMAIL
ANDREW WALKER
NIGEL WRIGHT

BETHANY HOUSE PUBLISHERS
Minneapolis, Minnesota 55438

130253

A C.S. Lewis Centre Book. First published in Great Britain under the title
Charismatic Renewal: The Search for a Theology 1993, by the Society for
Promoting Christian Knowledge, Holy Trinity Church, Marylebone Road,
London, MW1 4DU. U.K. edition edited by David Mackinder. U.S. edition
edited by Steven R. Laube.

Published by Bethany House Publishers
A Ministry of Bethany Fellowship, Inc.
11300 Hampshire Avenue South
Minneapolis, Minnesota 55438

Printed in the United States of America

Library of Congress Cataloging-in-Publication Data

Smail, Thomas Allan, 1928–
    [Charismatic renewal]
    The love of power or the power of love / Tom Smail, Andrew Walker,
Nigel Wright.
        p.   cm.
    Originally published: Charismatic renewal. London : Society for
Promoting Christian Knowledge, 1993.
    Includes bibliographical references.

    1. Pentecostalism.   2. Pentecostalism—Great Britain—Controversial
literature.   3. Wimber, John.   4. Faith movement (Hagin)—Controversial
literature.   5. Demonology—Controversial literature.   6. Church renewal.
7. Great Britain—Church history—20th century.   I. Walker, Andrew.
II. Wright, Nigel.   III. Title.   IV. Title: Power of love.
BR1644.S54   1993
270.8'2—dc20   94–4744
ISBN 1–55661–454–3 (pbk.)   CIP

Contents

―――

Introduction   *Tom Smail*   7

Part One: Charismatic Renewal—The Search for a Theology

1. The Cross and the Spirit: Toward a Theology of Renewal
   Tom Smail   13
2. The Theology of Signs and Wonders   *Nigel Wright*   37
3. Demonology and the Charismatic Movement
   Andrew Walker   53
4. The Faith Movement and the Question of Heresy
   Andrew Walker, Tom Smail, and Nigel Wright   73

Part Two: Issues for Renewal—Practical Considerations

5. In Spirit and in Truth: Reflections on Charismatic
   Worship   *Tom Smail*   95
6. The Rise of the Prophetic   *Nigel Wright*   105
7. Miracles As Holy: The Spirituality of
   the Unexplained   *Andrew Walker*   113

Part Three: Experiencing the Renewal

8. A Renewal Recalled   *Tom Smail*   125
9. A Pilgrimage in Renewal   *Nigel Wright*   141
10. Notes From a Wayward Son   *Andrew Walker*   153
Notes   169

Introduction

TOM SMAIL

Many more people have had a hand in the writing of this book than its three named authors. Most of its contents were first presented as papers at a weekend seminar organized by the C. S. Lewis Centre, with which all three of use are closely associated, under the title, *The Love of Power or the Power of Love—Reflecting on Charismatic Renewal*. To the best of our knowledge, this was the first gathering ever convened in Britain for this specific purpose, certainly by people who were basically sympathetic to the renewal. Those who attended, most of whom had active charismatic involvements of one kind or another, were so appreciative of and enthusiastic about the opportunity they were being offered that we were emboldened to repeat the experiment in different parts of the country.

The result is that six such seminars have been held across Britain and, as a result, the original material has been considerably modified in the light of the responses it evoked from those who attended, and as we became aware of what most concerns many contemporary charismatic leaders who work in local church situations rather than on the itinerant scene. It could, I think, also be said that our individual contributions were not entirely unaffected by having to listen six times to one another! We do want to acknowledge our debt to all who came and contributed. If any of them should read what follows, I hope they will feel that what they said at the seminars has been listened to and taken seriously.

For our part, the whole experience has provided solid and encouraging evidence that the charismatic renewal is at last entering a much more reflective phase, in which people are not simply content to worship with swaying bodies and closed eyes, but are becoming more ready—not before time—to take stock of how things have developed, what theology is implicit in charismatic attitudes, practices, and priorities, and how it squares with the biblical gospel and its teaching about the Holy Spirit and His work. This is a welcome sign that the movement is becoming confident enough to be self-critical and mature enough to exercise that gift of discernment which is one of the most necessary but most neglected gifts of the Spirit, and one which may have a good deal more to do with theological reflection than some charismatics may sometimes have supposed. It is to provide some additional stimulus to that process of discernment that we offer our material in this more permanent form.

What follows is divided into three parts, to each of which we have all three made our own contributions.

Part 1 contains the central theological reflections about the charismatic renewal in its current stage of development, which the three of us most want to offer both to our fellow participants in the renewal and to all our fellow Christians in the Church who want to know what to make of the renewal.

My own contribution is the most general and seeks for a theological understanding of renewal that will be faithful to the relationship between the renewing Spirit and the crucified Christ that the New Testament expounds and implies. Nigel Wright is more specific in his treatment of John Wimber, whose teaching and practice he uses as a base for exploring some of the practical challenges and theological questions that the contemporary renewal has to face. Andrew Walker, along another but closely connected tack, looks for an approach to demonology that will both do justice to what the New Testament teaches and avoid the paranoid obsessions and destructive exaggerations that can arise and have in fact arisen in this area in some sections of the renewal.

Lastly, the three of us tackle the difficult questions that arise from the current penchant, primarily in America, for the Word-of-Faith Movement. Our treatment may seem unyielding, but we hope it will bring a sense of balance to some crucial theological questions.

The shorter contributions in Part 2 were written specifically for this book and have not been presented at the seminars. They do, however, attempt to deal with three subjects that were consistently raised at the seminars as connected matters of considerable concern in renewal circles. I have written about charismatic worship and how I think it can best be developed. Nigel Wright discusses the gift of prophecy in particular relationship to the so-called Kansas City prophets, while Andrew Walker explores the connection between miraculous charismatic phenomena and Christian holiness.

In Part 3 we all speak very personally and give an account of how we came to be involved in the charismatic renewal and what it has meant to us over the years since that involvement began. In the publicity for one of the seminars, people were invited to share in "reflections on the charismatic renewal by three of its friends." That is exactly what we see ourselves to be. Those who read on will see that we do not shrink from some quite trenchant criticisms of some aspects of contemporary charismatic life and activity, but they are the criticisms of those who are the grateful beneficiaries of the renewal, whose lives and ministries have been deeply affected for good by what we have received from God through it and who, out of love and gratitude, want to see it living up to the purposes that God has for it and escaping from some of the dead ends into which it has been in danger of being trapped.

To read our three testimonies—because that is what they are—is to realize what very different people we are and by what very different routes we have traveled. My own journey from Scottish Presbyterianism to an Anglican Team Rectorship by way of Northern Ireland and the Fountain Trust is made to look rather tame and conventional by Nigel Wright's story of his conversion and his dramatic ministry in a Baptist church in northwest England, and we both bid fair to be outdone by Andrew Walker's story of his pilgrimage from Elim Pentecostalism through unbelieving agnosticism to Eastern Orthodoxy in its Russian form. Nevertheless, the three stories, for all their differences, have an underlying unity and bear a not unimpressive witness to the activity of the one Holy Spirit and His resourcefulness and unending creativity in doing His work and achieving His purposes in a variety of situations and in people of quite different temperaments and personalities.

We hope that our readers will find our treatment of these varied themes stimulating and helpful, but we also hope that they will find a certain unity of outlook and approach that pervades the way three very different people approach a large diversity of material. While we are each wholly responsible only for our own writing, we were conscious as we listened to one another, and as we joined in discussion of the points people raised, of a deep underlying agreement about how things stand and what should be done about them. We present our writing in the hope that, in spite of all our faults and inadequacies, the Spirit may indeed be able to speak significantly and creatively through what we have tried to say.

ONE

Charismatic Renewal—The Search for a Theology

ONE

The Cross and the Spirit: Toward a Theology of Renewal

TOM SMAIL

A Movement in Need of Theology

Dr. James Packer once described the charismatic renewal as a move-ment looking for a theology. If he had said that it was a movement desperately in *need* of a theology, I would have agreed with him straight away—but, *looking* for a theology, how I wish it were true!

It has perhaps been true of the renewal movement in Europe, es-pecially in Roman Catholic circles, where, from near the beginning, it has attracted to itself some first-rate thinkers, who have helped it to understand itself and what God was doing through it. We need only think of such eminent theologians as Herbert Mühlen in Germany and the late Yves Congar in France. The latter's three-volume work, trans-lated into English under the title *I Believe in the Holy Spirit*, and published by Geoffrey Chapman,[1] is one of the very best pieces of writing in the whole range of charismatic literature—learned and full of insight and perception, but warm and readable as well.

Unfortunately in Anglo-Saxon Protestant circles, it has not been so. On the whole, until recently, and with a few notable exceptions like Bishop John V. Taylor, Professor J.D.G. Dunn, and J. Rodman Williams, the theologians have not concerned themselves much with the renewal, and the renewal has certainly not been involved with the theologians. I can remember in the mid–1970s, in my early days with the Fountain Trust, if you said the word "theology" in a gathering of charismatic clergy, the chief reaction would be a scornful titter, as if they were saying, "Now that we have been renewed in the Spirit, we do not need to bother with that sort of thing anymore."

Most of the mainline denominations have also taken their time in subjecting the renewal to serious theological scrutiny. The exception was the Church of Scotland, whose Panel on Doctrine produced a significant report on the matter in the 1970s; but we had to wait till 1991 before the Doctrine Commission of the Church of England pro-duced a most welcome report, *We Believe in the Holy Spirit*,[2] which has at last subjected the renewal to a full and very helpful theological examination and appraisal.

This long-standing disjunction between spiritual renewal and aca-demic theology is, of course, not hard to understand. A great deal of Anglo-Saxon theology contemporary with the charismatic renewal has been, at best, taken up with very different issues and, at worst, has been based on liberal and even radical presuppositions that most participants in the renewal would find unacceptable and even destructive. It is easy to see why people should have reached the conclusion that, "If this is what theology is about, it has nothing to do with us," and even, "We want nothing to do with it."

In any case, it could be argued that charismatic renewal has to do with experience *of* God rather than thinking *about* God, and it is certainly true that its central contribution has been to emphasize once again the here and now activity in His Spirit of the God and Father of our Lord Jesus Christ. For charismatics, as for many others before them and alongside them, God is not an intellectual hypothesis to be discussed, but a living, personal Agent to be encountered. He is less the God of long words and sophisticated arguments, and more the God of contem-porary eventfulness, who touches and changes people and makes them new for himself. When that happens, either individually for people or corporately for churches, they easily come to the conclusion that they have neither need nor time for a complicated theology and all the awkward questions it insists on raising.

That impatience with theology in general and with much recent theology in particular is very easy to understand. As I shall later explain, part of my own preparation for renewal in the Spirit was to allow myself to be brought to a point where theological activity was for a time put into suspense; I stopped thinking about God in order that I could with open heart and mind meet Him and let Him begin to liberate me by His Spirit. But, just after my own experience of renewal had begun, I went to a gathering of classical Pentecostal leaders in a mining village in industrial Scotland, at which one of them said to me, "Be sure you hold on to your good theology. We have got into all sorts of trouble because we did not have it, and I can tell you from long experience that you are going to need it more than ever now."

How right he was! We need good theology for the same reason that we need good maps. Both are fascinating to people of a certain temperament, of whom, I admit, I am one. In the war years, when long-distance travel was largely impossible, I used to lie on my mother's lounge carpet and pore over every map I could get a hold of, even though I had no hope of actually going to any of the places that the maps depicted. However fascinating maps and theology may be in their different ways, neither is of much practical use if you are unable to move in the areas they delineate. However, both become quite indis-pensable when you start traveling and need to know where you are going and how you are going to get there.

A church that has gotten stuck, that lacks the motivation and energy to engage in the mission to which God has called it, may still be fasci-nated by theology in much the same way as I was fascinated by maps of places I had no means of visiting. The theology of such a church may be biblical and orthodox, but it is likely to be cold and largely detached from what it is actually living and experiencing. But when that church is touched by the renewing Spirit of God, so that it is now on the move in every area of its worship, fellowship, and mission, then indeed its good theology will be of the greatest use to it. For such a church, just because it is so full of life, needs to know what a good theology can help to tell it; where to go and how to get there, what is real and not real in its renewed life, and, when it is over-engrossed with one redis-covered aspect of the gospel, such as the gifts of the Spirit, to remind it that there are other aspects of the same gospel that it ignores at its peril. If you have a tiger in your tank, but no map for the journey, I am certainly not coming with you, for fear that we might end in the ditch or even in the mire!

Charismatics—and indeed all Christians who rightly give priority to the spiritual over the cerebral—need to learn that theology also has a spiritual dimension to it. It is not an intellectual optional extra for academics that other believers can safely ignore. In fact academics, if that is all they are, are likely to do their theology very badly, because they will lack personal participation in the things they are thinking about. Thinking about God is bound to remain remote, abstract, and woefully secondhand if you have no relationship with the God you are thinking about.

Nevertheless, it is equally important to recognize that an encounter with God in the Spirit is meant to engage our thoughts as well as our emotions, our minds as well as our hearts. Paul tells his Roman readers that if they are to know God's will and God's guidance they must, as part of their living sacrifice and their spiritual act of worship, offer their minds to be transformed and renewed: "I urge you, brothers, in view of God's mercy, to offer your bodies as living sacrifices . . . this is your spiritual act of worship. Do not conform any longer to the pattern of this world, *but be transformed by the renewing of your mind.* Then you will be able to test and approve what God's will is—his good, pleasing and perfect will" (Romans 12:1–2). Such a renewed mind will, as a direct result of the action of the Spirit upon it, begin to produce a charismatic theology.

In Search of a Charismatic Theology

Theological activity is, in fact, not so easily avoided as some of us would like to think, for there is no such a thing as a church or even a Christian without any theology. We may have picked it up from others, almost without realizing what we were doing, or we may have thought it through carefully for ourselves, with the result that it may influence us either at a highly conscious or at a largely unconscious level. It may be a theology shaped by the Scriptures, by the church tradition we have inherited, by the presuppositions of the secular society to which we belong, or, more likely, by a combination of all these factors and of many others besides. Always, however, the way we conduct our Christian

16

lives, the priorities we set, and the expectations we cherish will betray the fundamental theological conception of God on the basis of which we are operating. These attitudes show what we think God is like, what we think He will do for us, and what we think He is asking us to do for Him—the central concerns of any Christian theology.

Therefore the choice is never between theology and no theology, but is always about what kind of theology we are going to work with. Will it be consistent or inconsistent, will it be thought through for ourselves or merely picked up from others? How does it relate to the biblical gospel that we all believe and to the tradition of the church to which we belong? These are vital questions that none of us can afford to evade, and we need to think theologically in order to answer them.

Some of the beneficiaries of the charismatic renewal may still be indifferent to the need for theological reflection about it, but in the last few years there are welcome signs that attitudes are changing. Many thoughtful charismatics are now recognizing that there are grave dangers in allowing themselves to be affected and influenced by an unexamined theology, whose credentials they have never carefully scrutinized and which they are therefore not in a position to criticize or correct.

I am convinced that on the one hand the charismatic renewal has its origin in an authentic work of God the Holy Spirit, which is an important part of God's giving of himself to His people in our generation and is a situation which the Church ignores or rejects at its peril. But on the other hand, it is very important to see that that work of the Holy Spirit has been understood and interpreted largely in terms of a particular theological tradition, which stems from the Protestant Reformation, as modified by the pietist movement and Methodist holiness teaching and latterly by classical Pentecostalism. It was from that very specific matrix that the renewal reached us, and it bears the marks of its origin upon it still.

That explains my own ambiguous reaction to the renewal when I first encountered it in the person of Dennis Bennett in 1965. I discerned in him a genuine work of the Holy Spirit that made me aware of my own need, so that I began to wonder how I could share in what God had so obviously given him. At the same time, I could not help questioning the adequacy of the theological framework in which his new experience of God was presented. Bennett seemed quite uncritically to have taken over Pentecostal theology along with Pentecostal experience, and my own commitment to reformed Calvinism made it impossible for me to do the same.

The point I want to make is that we need to distinguish between the wonderful works of God among His people and the theological traditions by which we try to interpret them. The genuineness and efficacy of the Spirit's work by no means guarantees the adequacy of the theology by which we try to grasp its meaning. All our theological traditions need to be recognized for what they are—interpretations of the gospel that do justice to some aspects of it and fail to do justice to others. They all need to be submitted afresh to the fullness of God's truth as it is revealed in Christ and witnessed in the Scriptures, so that all our theologies can be corrected by the living Word of God. As part of this task, we need to listen to one another across the theological divisions in the Church so that we may bring into focus what others have seen more clearly than we and, at the same time, help them by the insights that have been central for us.

Like all other theologies, the Pentecostal theology, in which the charismatic renewal has been cradled and by which it has been shaped, needs, with the help of the other Christian traditions, to be exposed to the whole range of gospel truth, in order that we may see where it is adequate to that truth and where it is quite inadequate to it.

Its adequacies in comparison with other longer established traditions must be recognized and upheld; we have had, and still have, much to learn from the Pentecostals. Their distinctive approach to the gospel has brought into sharp focus aspects of the Holy Spirit's work, which much Catholic and Protestant teaching, including that of my own reformed tradition, has at worst suppressed and at best ignored. The Pentecostals have reminded us that to be a Christian is not just to be a sinner justified by grace, not just to embark on the long process of sanctifying moral transformation into the likeness of Christ; it is also to be empowered by the Holy Spirit and endowed with His many and varied gifts for the mission to the world to which Christ has called all His people. No one in our century has drawn attention to what the New Testament says in this regard more emphatically than the Pentecostals, and we owe them a great debt of gratitude for refocusing our attention and expectation on a part of our heritage in Christ that had been neglected in the mainline churches, certainly in the West.

At the same time, however, we need to recognize that Pentecostal theology, like all other Christian traditions, has its own limitations. Chief among these, in my view, is the fact that the basic structures of Pentecostal theology make it difficult to recognize the close and intimate relationship between the renewing and empowering work of the Spirit and the center of the gospel in the incarnation, death, and resurrection of Jesus Christ. Such a failure involves not just a theological imbalance between different aspects of the gospel, but is at the root of many of the practical exaggerations and aberrations with which, it seems to me, some sections of the renewal movement are currently threatened.

We are indeed rejuvenated and empowered at Pentecost, but we are judged, corrected, and matured at the cross; and for these two processes to be brought into right relationship with each other, we must, I believe, understand the relation between cross and Spirit in a way that is quite different from the way it is understood by the Pentecostal theology that has shaped the renewal until now. That is my basic thesis in this chapter, and I go on now to expound it in greater detail and to show what some of its practical implications are.

For me the clue to all this goes back to my own early charismatic days in the mid–1960s. Just a few months after my own renewal experience, I went to a small conference in Crieff, Perthshire, for ministers who were interested or involved. There, for the first time, I dared to exercise in public the gift of tongues that I had recently received. The interpretation was given by a young woman, and I have never forgotten what she said, "The way to Pentecost is Calvary; the Spirit comes from the cross." That, in a sentence, has been at the center of my own thinking about Christian renewal ever since, and it could well stand as a text for all that follows.

It is of course a statement with which no Christian, of whatever tradition, could possibly disagree, Pentecostal Christians least of all; but my contention is that the whole shape of Pentecostal theology makes it difficult for the full meaning of that statement to be properly recognized. To explain what I mean, it will be helpful to distinguish and contrast two models of renewal, the one which we will call the Pentecostal model and the other the Paschal model, each of which we can now outline in turn.

The Pentecostal Model

According to the Pentecostal model, Christian renewal is to be understood primarily and centrally in terms of what happened on the Day of Pentecost, which is seen as the second of the two great New Testament beginnings that God made with His people. The first is the coming of Jesus to live as man, to die for our salvation, and to rise again. It starts at Christmas, it ends with a withdrawal of Jesus at His ascension, and it is followed by the second stage, the coming of the Holy Spirit in the dramatic experience of Pentecost, to empower the Church for its mission, to equip it with His gifts, and to sanctify it with His fruit.

The Pentecostal reception of the Spirit is seen in some sense as the goal and end of the whole Christian enterprise. The work of Christ is indeed a necessary and indispensable preparation for it; we shall not get there without Jesus and the cross; but to enter into Pentecost is to pass beyond the cross into a new supernatural world in which center stage is held not by the incarnate, crucified, and risen Lord, but by the Spirit and the dramatic manifestations of His triumphant power.

There is of course in all this no intention to break or even diminish the connection between Jesus and the Spirit. Indeed it is explicitly taught that it is Jesus who baptizes His people with His own Spirit. Nevertheless, the saving activity of Jesus on the cross and the Pentecostal activity of the Holy Spirit do tend to be segregated into different compartments. The first relates to what Jesus did for us long ago, and therefore its norms are more biblical; the second relates to what the Spirit is doing here and now, and its norms are more experiential. Much preaching and teaching in the renewal nowadays—perhaps in contrast with its earlier beginnings—consist more of testimonies to and anecdotes about the present-day works of the Spirit than of expositions of the Word of Scripture. The attendant danger is that contemporary experience will be valued more highly than biblical truth, and that what God is doing by His Spirit will be less and less related to what He has once-for-all done for us in His Son.

That is borne out when one comes across charismatic people whose whole talk is of words of knowledge, of deliverances from evil, being slain in the Spirit, of tingling hands and high emotions at great charismatic gatherings, till one is left wondering to what extent such preoccupations bring us nearer to the heart of the New Testament gospel and to what extent they distract and divert us from it. These may be extreme cases, but they do illustrate the dangers that beset us when our claims to experience of the Spirit are not related in the closest possible way to God's final and normative revelation of himself in the life, death, and resurrection of Christ.

For the Pentecostal model, the two successive stages of God's New Testament activity, first in Jesus and then in the Spirit, are reflected in a two-stage model of Christian initiation, both of which are entered by a decisive crisis experience. First we are converted to Christ and are pardoned at the cross, and then later we are baptized in the Spirit and begin to manifest His power by speaking in tongues or by the exercise of some other spiritual gift.

Such a presentation of the gospel is open to a whole host of biblical, theological, and pastoral objections, which have been much discussed in recent years. The objection that is relevant to our present subject is the compartmentalism that this way of looking at things entails. To put it simply, the cross is located in the pardon department; it is the place where our Christian life begins when we come as sinners seeking God's pardon, and it is the place to which we return again and again when we need to be forgiven.

Beyond the cross, at the second stage of our Christian initiation, is the power department, over which the Spirit presides and which we enter at our personal Pentecost. Although the pardon department and the power department are undoubtedly under the same Christian roof, what happens in the one need have no essential relationship with what happens in the other, and, as we shall see, there is a real danger that we shall begin to speak about the power of the Spirit in ways that are at variance with—even in contradiction to—the gospel of the cross.

Furthermore, it is clear that the second Pentecostal stage in this scheme is seen as an advance upon and superior to the first. Christians who know only Christ crucified and have not yet gone on to be baptized in the Holy Spirit are adjudged to be ill-equipped and largely ineffectual, because they have failed to appropriate the Spirit's power. They are accordingly exhorted to repent, believe, tarry, and claim the promise until the moment comes when they are initiated into the second stage and know the fullness of the Spirit and His gifts.

So to put it, the gospel of the cross can easily come to be seen as a kind of beginning level Christianity through which you must pass in order to graduate to the advanced level of charismatic experience. One of the chief dangers of such an approach is that charismatic experience can become an autonomous realm of its own, where we no longer ask how our experiences and our expectations square with the gospel of Christ crucified. Bolstered up by what has happened to us and by the testimonies of others, we can easily come to see ourselves as living in a world of supernatural power that leads us from triumph to triumph, where the weak, desolate sufferer of Calvary has been left far behind, or at any rate has ceased to dominate the scene.

It was through this kind of teaching that many of us became aware of new dimensions of the gospel of which we had been largely unaware, and we must therefore always speak of it with gratitude and respect, but that should not prevent us from recognizing its dangers and deficiencies and from looking for an alternative model that will conserve all that is good in the Pentecostal model but without its tendency to separate renewal in the Spirit from salvation by the cross.

Martin Luther used to contrast what he called *theologia crucis*, the theology of the cross that was centered on the crucified Jesus, with *theologia gloriae*, the theology of glory that tried to deal with God in a way that did not take the cross fully into account. He knew very well that our sinful hearts are forever devising ways of evading the cross, because it is there that we are most radically judged in order that we may be most radically forgiven, and most deeply humbled in order that we may be most highly exalted. In our present context, therefore, we need to be on constant guard, in case, without any conscious intention, we should begin to evade the cross by devising and promoting a charismatic theology of glory. A spirit who diverts us from the cross into a triumphant world in which the cross does not hold sway may turn out to be a very *un*holy spirit.

The Pentecostal model of renewal we have been outlining often seeks its biblical basis in Luke's gospel and its sequel in the Acts of the

Apostles. It would be quite wrong to suggest that Luke held anything like a two-stage Pentecostal theology of initiation; but it is true that for Luke Calvary and Pentecost were two separate events with over six weeks between them. At the end of the Lukan forty days Jesus withdraws, promising that the Spirit will come, as indeed He does, ten days later, in dramatic Pentecostal signs and wonders. It is also true that Luke is less interested in the meaning of the cross than in the first days of the Church and its mission. To that extent Pentecostals are not entirely mistaken in claiming him as their best New Testament friend.

The Paschal Model

If, however, we are looking for a more adequate model, we shall find it when we turn from Luke—first to John and then to Paul, for it is in their writings that we can clearly see the alternative Pashcal model beginning to emerge.

At various points throughout his gospel, John hints at the close connection between the passion of Jesus and the coming of the Spirit. At the very beginning, the Jesus on whom the Spirit is seen to descend and rest at the Jordan, and who will baptize others with that same Spirit, is the very Jesus who has just been hailed as the sacrificial lamb of God who will take away the sin of the world (John 1:29–33). The coming of the Spirit, so clearly promised in the farewell discourses, is dependent on the *going away* of Jesus—John's comprehensive term for His death, His rising, and His ascension: "Unless I *go away*, the Counselor will not come to you; but if I go, I will send him to you" (16:7).

It is, however, in John's passion and resurrection narratives that the connection between cross and Spirit is most clearly indicated. So in John 19:30, "When Jesus had received the vinegar he bowed his head and *handed over the Spirit*" (translation mine). The Greek of that phrase certainly means that in His last moment He surrendered His spirit to His Father (i.e., He died), and that is the usual translation. But there is good authority among both ancient and contemporary commentators for holding that it can also mean that He bowed His head toward the little group at the foot of the cross, representing as they did the final moment of the old Israel and the first promise of the new, and handed over His Spirit to them. The Spirit is the Spirit of Calvary; the power by which He works is the same kind of power by which Jesus defeated the powers of evil by sharing our suffering and shouldering our sin on the cross. Here the coming of the Spirit is not postponed till Pentecost; ". . . the Spirit comes from the cross."

The same point is underlined a little later in the same chapter, where, in John 19:34–35, there comes from the pierced side of Jesus "a sudden flow of blood and water," which the writer emphasizes, because it symbolizes what has been accomplished by the Lord's death. One has only to remember Jesus' words to the woman at the well in John 4:13–14, and His promise of streams of living water to those who come to Him thirsty in 7:37–38, and its interpretation as a promise of the Spirit in verse 39, to realize that in this gospel water is always a symbol of the Spirit, so that to say that water flows from the wounded side of the crucified Jesus is yet another way of telling us that the Spirit comes from the cross.

So also in the resurrection story of John 20:19–23. On Easter evening the risen Christ, who has just shown His disciples His hands and side that still bear the wounds of the cross, breathes His Spirit upon them. This is of tremendous importance, as we shall see later. The risen Christ is still the crucified Christ. His passion is not left behind Him, the marks of His suffering, far from being removed, are the very stuff out of which His risen glory is fashioned. It is these crucified hands that are stretched out to impart the Spirit, and that Spirit is given to impart not primarily charismatic gifts, but rather the peace with God that comes through sins forgiven, which is the gift of the cross. "He breathed on them and said, 'Receive the Holy Spirit. If you forgive anyone his sins, they are forgiven' " (20:22–23).

For John, it is not enough to say that the Spirit comes after and as a result of the death and resurrection of Jesus, as in the Pentecostal model. In this gospel the way of the cross and the way of the Spirit are one and the same. The Spirit leads us as He led Jesus, to glory fashioned in suffering, to victory won through defeat, to power exercised in weakness, to a throne that is the same shape as a cross. This Spirit will never lead us away from or past the cross of Christ; rather, He will constantly bring us back to it, because it is the one source of that strange power by which God through Christ has overcome the world.

This is the Pashcal model of Christian renewal. According to it the

cross and resurrection of Jesus are the saving center of all God's dealings
with us, and all that He does in us by His Spirit will proceed from His
passion and His rising and be conformed to them. There are not two
circles, one with the cross at its center and another with the Spirit at
its center, but only one circle with the crucified and risen Lord at its
center. It is to Him that the Father has given the Spirit, and it is by Him
that the Spirit is given to His people, as the Spirit of His passion and
only so as the Spirit of His power.

When we turn from John to Paul, we find a similar awareness of
the connection between the cross and the Spirit. In the first two chapters of 1 Corinthians, Paul takes issue both with Greeks who want an
intellectually respectable theology and Jews who want sweeping demonstrations of supernatural power, signs and wonders that manifest
God's presence in sensational and dramatic ways. Both Greek ration-
alists and Jewish supernaturalists are bound to resist Paul's gospel of
the cross, because it fulfills neither of these requirements. "Jews demand
miraculous signs and Greeks look for wisdom, but we preach Christ
crucified: a stumbling block to Jews and foolishness to Gentiles, but to
those whom God has called . . . Christ the power of God and the wisdom
of God. For the foolishness of God is wiser than man's wisdom, and
the weakness of God is stronger than man's strength" (1 Corinthians
1:22–25); and again, "I resolved to know nothing while I was with you
except Jesus Christ and him crucified" (2:2).

That does not, of course, mean that the only subject Paul will talk
to the Corinthians about is the cross. The remainder of the letter gives
ample evidence to the contrary. Far from being excluded, there is a
whole chapter about the Resurrection (Ch. 15), but it is seen as first
and foremost the resurrection of the crucified Jesus. The Spirit and His
gifts have no less than four chapters of this letter (Chs. 11–14), and just
a few verses further on in the passage we have been considering he
tells us that "My message and my preaching [with the cross as their
subject and center] were not with wise and persuasive words, but with
a demonstration of the Spirit's power, so that your faith might not rest
on men's wisdom, but on God's power" (2:4–5).

Paul, unlike some contemporary radical theologians, is not promul-
gating some theory of God's arbitrariness and impotence. He is as
interested in rationality and power as his Greek and Jewish adversaries.

But for him, paradoxically, wisdom and power are located in the seemingly senseless and powerless suffering of Jesus on the cross. The power that is exercised from the cross is for Paul the mightiest power in all creation, and it is given proof of itself in Corinth, where his preaching of the weak and crucified Jesus has gathered the Corinthian congregation, in which there has been ample evidence of the Spirit's charismatic activity. This passage, far from repudiating charismatic power, strongly affirms it, but it is the sort of power that comes from the cross and is released by the message of the cross. Once again Paul is using a cross-centered Paschal model by which to interpret the work of the Holy Spirit.

The Love of Power or the Power of Love

In the light of all this, I am not sure quite what to make of some recent teaching about the power of the Holy Spirit. In the wake of John Wimber, there has been much talk about power evangelism, power healing, and power encounters with the forces of evil, and we need to ask carefully what exactly it means.

Insofar as this power language is just another way of insisting that we are still to look for and expect what Paul calls demonstrations of the Spirit's power, it is making a point that is totally acceptable and has much New Testament support. To take Christ seriously, people need to know that His promises are being kept and that He is still at work among us by His Spirit, so that, for those who have eyes to see, there is contemporary evidence of His healing and liberating power.

What gives me concern, however, is that, if we are not careful, it is just at this point that wrong notions about the power of God can easily creep in. An uncritical and unqualified use of power language can easily give the impression that we think that God deals with evil in all its forms by unleashing against it a violent onslaught of superior supernatural force, by which it is immediately crushed and subdued. We can use militaristic language in a very naive way which suggests that the goodies have better weapons that the baddies, that all they need to do is to equip themselves with the supernatural energy and gifts of the Spirit and may then expect to advance from triumph to triumph in His overwhelming power. That is no doubt an exaggeration of this kind of teaching, but it does, I believe, identify one tendency within it that sets my alarm bells ringing. It sounds far too much like that cross-evading *theologia gloriae*, against which Luther warned so sternly, and it is very far from faithful to what the New Testament has to say about God's power and the way it is exercised in Christ.

In other words, if we talk power language too glibly, we are in danger of forgetting that the power of Jesus and therefore the power of the Spirit that Jesus gave us are not like that at all. Jesus did not attack evil by standing outside it in divine immunity and smashing it with the laser beams of supernatural force; He did not defeat it by violent and overwhelming assault upon it, but rather by taking it on himself and letting it do its worst to Him. He freed sinners by sharing the consequences of their sin with them; He delivered sufferers by a costly identification with them in their suffering, in self-giving that poured itself out for them and to them and in that way healed and helped them.

When we take our bearings from the cross, we can see that the only power with which Jesus works is the power of that utterly self-giving love that was itself weak and helpless on Calvary. He overcame all the violent force and energy of evil that fell upon Him there, not by exercising greater force and violence, but by renouncing them altogether. The power of Jesus, and therefore the power of the Spirit that Jesus imparts from the cross, is the power of Calvary love. It is by that love—nothing more and nothing less—that God delivers, remakes, heals, frees, and saves.

Most significantly, it is at the point where he is recording the remarkable effectiveness of the healing ministry of Jesus that Matthew quotes, as a commentary on what he has just been describing, the passage about the suffering servant of God from Isaiah 53. So Matthew 8:16–17 says, "When evening came, many who were demon-possessed were brought to him, and he drove out the spirits with a word and healed all the sick. This was to fulfill what was spoken through the prophet Isaiah: 'He took up our infirmities and carried our diseases.'"

The healing ministry of Jesus does not operate by the hurtling of irresistible divine force against demonic evil. The word that drives out the demons is the word of the suffering servant who bears our sins, shares our sufferings, and carries our diseases. He can do what He does because He is on His way to the cross; He is moving ever further into His costly identification with us, taking on himself what is destroying us, penetrating by His love into the very heart of what is wrong with us, and so sharing His own wholeness with us.

What heals is not esoteric techniques, or even special supernatural endowments as such; what heals is Calvary love. The charismatic renewal strays furthest from its own best insights and becomes most nearly gnostic in its seemingly endless search for the effective technique, the method, the panacea that will release the power of God to deal with all the ills of His people. The sesame key to wholeness is not speaking in tongues, or the healing of the memories, thanking God for everything or asking Him for anything; it is not having your demons cast out, still less being "slain" in the Spirit or reliving your traumatic birth experience, or any other of the fashions that have followed one another in quite fast succession over the past twenty-five years. All these can at best offer subsidiary assistance to some people in some situations, but the ultimate key to the wholeness that God purposes for His people and His world is far more central to the gospel than any of these; it is Calvary love.

A church in which healing, renewal, and effective evangelism can happen is a church that is open to receive Christ's Calvary love, to demonstrate it in specific ways in the relationships of its members to one another, and to extend it to those outside its own fellowship with whom it comes into contact. Such a church will get near to people by its acceptance of them and will intercede for people in a way that takes its inspiration from the kind of intercession that Jesus made when He identified himself on the cross with the sinners and sufferers of the world and offered himself to God on their behalf.

Where there is little healing and renewal among us, it is not chiefly because we have not entered into the appropriate spiritual experiences or not been open to the needed charismatic gifts; rather, it is because we have been lacking in this quality of love. What we need to seek from the Spirit, much more than any of the gifts that charismatics have valued so highly, is, as Paul puts it in Romans 5:5, that God should "[pour] out his love into our hearts by the Holy Spirit, whom he has given us." God's healing and renewing power is not something other than or apart from that love; that love itself is the most powerful thing on earth and in heaven. By it, through it, and for it God made the world, and by it, through it, and for it He has saved and begun to renew the world in Christ. The spiritual gifts are wholesome and upbuilding only if they are received and exercised as *charismata*, the specific and appropriate expressions of that gracious love of which the Greek word speaks; without it they soon become dangerous and disruptive.

If some of us who have been charismatic leaders had been as set on being filled with the love of God as we have been on being filled with the power of God, the charismatic renewal would be a more unambiguously wholesome affair than it has sometimes been; not so many people who have been blessed through it would also have to say that they have been hurt by it. The Spirit can use a Christian community that has begun to love even a little in the way Jesus loved on the cross far more than He can use people who may have sensational experiences and dramatic gifts in plenty, but who do not know how to love in this way.

All this is, of course, good 1 Corinthians 13 teaching, which we ignore or play down at our peril. That chapter tells us clearly what Paul most needed to say to the Corinthian charismatics, and it still needs, more than anything else, to be said to contemporary charismatics. We too may speak with the tongues of men and of angels, we may have prophetic gifts and claim to fathom God's mysteries, we may have all kinds of detailed words of knowledge and a faith that expects and sometimes achieves the most extraordinary results, but if, having all these, we do not also have the love in which Jesus died on Calvary, in God's eyes it all counts for nothing at all. When Jesus bowed His head on the cross and handed over the Spirit, it was the Spirit of this love that He gave.

It is such insights into the nature of the Holy Spirit's power that come into much sharper focus when we think of the Spirit in terms of the Paschal rather than the Pentecostal model, because now cross and Spirit, love and power are not segregated in separate compartments, but are held together in the closest possible identity with each other.

Toward a Theology of Suffering

There is, however, another whole area in which the Paschal model has much to offer. As well as opening up, as we have just been seeing, a fresh approach to renewal and healing in their relationship to Christ's cross, it also makes possible a new understanding of unrelieved suffering and failure to heal. These are always a great problem for the Pentecostal model, which is exposed to constant temptation to a glib triumphalism that arouses in people expectations which it is only sometimes able to fulfill, with the sad result that many people are left in deep guilt because they did not have enough faith to be healed, or else in disillusionment because the promises so confidently made to them have not been kept.

When we expose this whole dark area to the light that comes from the cross and resurrection of Jesus, we can begin to see that God's purpose in such situations is not always to take us *out* of what is threatening to hurt or destroy us, but is sometimes rather to take us *through* it. Our ultimate victory comes not from escaping evil but from being given the ability to endure and bear it, the way that Jesus bore it on the cross, so that the death that was its ultimate destructive onslaught upon Him became the way to His own Easter victory and to the world's salvation.

When God's own self-giving love gets into the midst of a situation dominated by sin, suffering, and death, the way it did with Jesus on the cross, it acts creatively and transformingly on that situation. What is in itself totally destructive can become, by Christ's presence in it, salvific and redemptive. Christ does not rise on Easter day *in spite of* His sufferings and death, but rather *because of* them. The risen Jesus is still the wounded Jesus; in His resurrection He does not leave His passion behind Him; He bears the marks of it still in His body and displays them as the trophies of His triumph. His suffering is the very stuff out of which He fashions His glory.

The New Testament makes it clear that the way of the Master is the way of the disciple. He calls us to take up our cross and follow Him. That means that we have no guarantee of immunity either from the kind of suffering that is a direct consequence of our discipleship or from the accidents, misfortunes, illnesses, and disabilities that afflict other people and are as liable to afflict us as well. Paul was imprisoned in Philippi as a direct result of his Christian witness there (Acts 16:23), but equally the ship on which he sailed for Rome was not spared the storm and the shipwreck that were the normal risk of all Mediterranean seafarers at that time of year (Acts 27). He was rescued from neither persecution nor misfortune, but was brought through both to fresh opportunities for the gospel.

So for Christians today there come times when Jesus calls us to follow Him in the way of the cross, where the delivering signs and wonders do not happen, where the trouble from which we pray to be freed is neither removed nor alleviated, but becomes the material out of which God fashions us into richer and deeper realms of renewal, which, looking back, we see could not have been reached in any other way.

Very relevant to all this is the saying of C. S. Lewis, "Miracles are for beginners." I take this to mean that, when we are in the early stages of the Christian life, where faith most needs to be confirmed and built up, God will often show himself to be the rescuer, who gets us out of our trouble. When, however, we become stronger and more mature, He will often honor us, not by giving us the deliverances we ask, but by calling us to follow Jesus through the dark, even deadly places where no relief comes, to the new life that lies on the other side of whatever Jordan of suffering and affliction we have to cross. And, of course, none of us will in the end escape the ultimate Jordan of death, which is the only access to the final glory that awaits us.

We need not take too literally the time-scale implied by the Lewis dictum. It is not only at the start of the Christian life that faith and confidence need to be built up, and God's wonderful rescuing deliverances can come at any time and in any situation, as in His wisdom and freedom He may choose. Nevertheless, Christian growth toward maturity comes less from seeing miracles than from being taken through suffering and learning to trust God to work out His good purposes in and through what we have to endure. If we can see Him at work only when we are rescued from evil, and cannot trust Him when the signs cease and the wonders do not happen we shall be in danger of remaining permanently in the Christian nursery instead of learning, as Paul put it to Timothy, "[to] endure hardship . . . like a good soldier of Christ Jesus" (2 Timothy 2:3).

The New Testament paradigm for all this is undoubtedly the way Paul understands what he calls his thorn in the flesh in 2 Corinthians 12:7–9. Much ink has been spilled in trying to identify what exactly he was talking about, and commentators have suggested everything from epileptic fits and eye trouble to the harrying of persecuting Jews. That debate is bound to be without conclusion since the relevant evidence is almost entirely lacking.

Nevertheless, Paul does tell us quite clearly that, whatever the precise nature of his trouble may have been, it was something that on the face of it fulfilled no obvious useful purpose. It gave him continual pain and played into the hands of Satan by at least partially disabling him from doing what God had called him to do. That much can be inferred from 12:7, "There was given me a thorn in the flesh, a messenger of Satan to torment me."

Paul's response to this situation was to pray that he should be set free from this disability, and to persist in this prayer when its request was not immediately granted. "Three times I pleaded with the Lord to take it away from me" (v. 8). The answer to that prayer, when at length it came, was a very specific refusal of the deliverance he asked for. To put it in current charismatic jargon, Paul was given a word of knowledge to the effect that he was to live with his affliction and not expect to be freed from it.

God was going to lead him by the way of the cross, by not rescuing him from the trouble, but by using it to bring him into even closer dependence upon himself. Paul had had sensational spiritual experiences, which he hints at in the verses immediately before this passage, and there was a danger that he might be carried away by them, so as to depend on them rather than the God who gave them—always a temptation for those who have had charismatic experiences, even of a much lesser kind. In such circumstances he needed his affliction to drive him back continually on his dependence on God. "But he said to me, 'My grace is sufficient for you, for my power is made perfect in weakness' " (v. 9). A disabled apostle depending on God is far more usable than a healthy apostle living out of his own spiritual capital.

It is as if God had said to him, "Your thorn in the flesh must remain, for although Satan put it there, I can use it to make you keep relying on me and so to outwit Satan. For when you rely on me in your woundedness, you are far more powerful in my service than if you were brimming with physical health, psychological balance, and spiritual self-sufficiency." The way that Paul goes on shows how well he has learned that hard lesson: "Therefore I will boast all the more gladly about my weaknesses, so that Christ's power may rest on me. That is why, for Christ's sake, I delight in weaknesses, in insults, in hardships, in persecutions, in difficulties. For when I am weak, then I am strong" (vv. 9–10).

"My power is made perfect in weakness"; "When I am weak, then I am strong." Those who understand what is happening to them in these terms are those who have entered deeply into the mystery of the strange power that God in Christ exercises from the apparent powerlessness of the cross. They know that when we assess these things in terms of a *theologia crucis*, weakness and power, suffering and triumph, defeat and victory, rejection and acceptance, death and resurrection are not contradictory but complementary, impossible as that may seem from any other standpoint.

As the Church of England Doctrine Commission report *We Believe in the Holy Spirit* puts it, "Jesus and his passion represent for us the touchstone of the power of which we speak, its effects when poured out, and its confrontation with other concepts of power abroad in the world."[3] In other words, God's power is understood in accordance with what we have been calling the Paschal model, it is the power of the cross, of the crucified and risen Lord.

That is why Paul can cope with God's refusal to remove his thorn in the flesh. He has learned at the cross not just about a rescuing God who takes people out of trouble but about a saving God who can use their trouble for their remaking, just as He used the awful suffering of Jesus for the remaking of the world. The Pentecostal model can offer us a theology of healing and triumph, but it cannot provide the basis for a theology of suffering and failure, which we need just as much. For that we have to turn, with Paul in his own suffering, to the Paschal model, with its center in the cross.

Renewal in the Spirit and Sharing the Cross

Far from advancing beyond the cross when we are renewed in the Spirit, needing to return to it only when we sin and need pardon, the Paschal model shows us that the more we are filled with the Spirit, the more we shall share in both cross and resurrection, again and again. The triumphalistic expectations of uninterrupted release and constant victory which the more naive part of the charismatic constituency has sometimes cherished and even taught are contradicted by both Scripture and experience alike.

For our New Testament example of this we need only remember Stephen, who is introduced to us in Acts 6 as a man "full of faith and of the Holy Spirit" (v. 5) and "full of God's grace and power" (v. 8)—a model charismatic indeed! Precisely because he was so full of the Spirit, Stephen saw that the gospel of Christ could not be contained within the bounds of Jewish exclusivism, but that through it God was moving out in grace from Israel to the whole Gentile world. Such a message roused against him a murderous Jewish opposition that contrived his stoning, just as it had contrived the crucifixion of Jesus. But because the Spirit who filled Stephen was the Spirit who had filled Jesus on the cross, he met his death in the same forgiving love to his enemies and trust in God, so that the last words of the martyr echo the last words of the master: "Lord, do not hold this sin against them" (7:60); "Lord Jesus, receive my spirit" (7:59).

But as death and defeat were not the end of the story for Jesus, neither were they for Stephen. Luke tells Stephen's story in a way that brings out quite clearly how his tragedy was used to bring about his triumph both in heaven and on earth. We are told how in the midst of his suffering he had a charismatic vision of the glory that awaited him with God: "I see heaven open and the Son of Man standing at the right hand of God" (Luke 7:56). Professor William Manson used to point out to his Edinburgh students that this is the only place in the New Testament where the exalted Lord is said to *stand* at the Father's right hand. In all other references he is said to *sit*, because sitting is the attitude of regnant majesty. But when the martyr who has followed the Lord all the way to the death comes, to receive him and to honor him the Son of Man rises from His throne. Almost, "Stand up, stand up for Stephen!" That is indeed triumph in heaven.

But there is triumph for Stephen and all that he died for here on earth as well. Luke tells us that "Meanwhile, the witnesses [to Stephen's stoning] laid their clothes at the feet of a young man named Saul" (7:58), who was soon also due to meet the exalted Lord on the road to Damascus. There he would be asked why he was continuing to kick against the pricks, why, in other words, he was resisting the growing conviction that, in persecuting the Christians, he was persecuting their Lord. If we ask what had begun to shake him in his old hostility and prepare him for his coming conversion, the answer, at which Luke at least hints, is that it was the way Stephen died.

Thus the death of Stephen was a powerful factor in initiating the taking of the gospel to the Gentile world through Paul. The very thing for which the martyr had died was beginning to happen in a way and to an extent of which he could never have dared to dream. Stephen moves from being filled with the Spirit to a sharing of the cross, and through that sharing of the cross to triumph both with God in heaven and with God's mission here on earth. That is the Paschal pattern of Christian life in the Spirit.

That pattern prevails equally in the more restricted world of the spiritual gifts in which modern charismatics are most interested. Mother Basileia Schlink of the Evangelical Sisterhood of Mary used to say that all the gifts of the Spirit are marked with the sign of the cross. To exercise a ministry of healing involves suffering with those who suffer and having to bear all the insoluble mysteries of why one is healed and another is not. Furthermore, if we desire to prophesy, we had better remember all the biblical evidence that the popularity rating and indeed the life-expectancy of authentic prophets has never been high!

Conclusions

It is time to summarize our conclusions. The central thrust of the argument has been that renewal in the Spirit urgently requires a theology that will do justice to all that is involved in it—a map of the journey to God's land of promise that has clearly marked on it both the power and the love, the failure and the triumph, the weakness and the strength, the suffering and the healing, the dying and the rising again. We have tried to show that a theology that will more adequately fulfil all these requirements will be one that has at its center not the experience of Pentecost only, but the Paschal mystery of the death and resurrection of Jesus, to which the Spirit who came to the Church at Pentecost bears witness in all His works and ways.

Of course, no theology can ever be finally adequate to the uncontrollable Spirit, who, as John reminds us, blows, like the wind, wherever

He pleases (John 3:8); but in all His incalculable freedom He remains the Spirit whom the Father gave to us through the Son who was to die and rise again. That is why the Spirit can so often be seen to be working within the rhythm of Christ's cross and resurrection.

Paul says all that I have been trying to say in Philippians 3:10, where he delineates the shape of the only renewal in the Spirit that at the end of the day matters: "I want to know Christ and the power of his resurrection and the fellowship of sharing in his sufferings, becoming like him in his death, and so, somehow, to attain to the resurrection from the dead."

TWO

The Theology of Signs and Wonders

NIGEL WRIGHT

One of the most significant movements over the last decade of the charismatic movement has been that associated with John Wimber, the leader of the California-based Vineyard Ministries.[1] A former rock musician and businessman, Wimber was for a time after his conversion pastor of an Evangelical Friends church in Orange County before becoming involved in the charismatic renewal and rising to prominence as an innovative and creative figure. He combined his ministry with part-time teaching at the Fuller Theological Seminary School of Church Growth and developed an approach to church growth known as "signs and wonders," the belief that it is the demonstration of the Spirit's power through healing and "power encounters" with the forces of darkness which is the most significant factor in the growth of the Church today, as it was in the early church. The penetration of this new movement into the historic churches has been described by Dr. Peter Wagner as the "Third Wave," subsequent to the emergence of Pentecostalism in the first decade of the century and of the charismatic movement in the 1960s. This chapter is concerned with an evaluation of some of the central claims and practices of the signs and wonders movement.

It is beyond dispute that Wimber's influence has been considerable, although now, for various reasons, it is in relative decline. In the early phases of the ministry, from 1981 onward, he imparted some new influence into the contemporary scene.

Although the charismatic movement had often talked the language of spiritual power, it was not until the advent of Wimber that such power was greatly in evidence. Early visits of Vineyard teams were characterized by definite outpourings of the Spirit, accompanied by unusual phenomena such as trembling, falling, trances, weeping, unrestrained laughter, and the release of anguish and pain in a startling and sometimes frightening fashion. Great emphasis was laid upon healing, the impartation of this gift sometimes being indicated by tingling sensations and warmth in the hands and arms. These occasions were intense, dramatic and yet, paradoxically, at the same time restrained. Emotionalism was firmly discouraged, and curbed as inimical to the Spirit. There was a great attraction, even to conservative church people, in intense religious experience, actual "demonstration" of the Spirit, being imparted within a disciplined framework.

A further element was the evident desire to "equip the saints," that is, to enable others to minister in the power of the Holy Spirit. This must be seen in contrast to the inclination in other charismatic leaders to be the center of attention, ministering powerfully in the anointing of the Spirit as the gifted among the ungifted. Wimber's intention was to break away from this, to enable and empower all and any to be used by God. This involved the impartation of spiritual anointing to others through prayer and touch, and the teaching of methodologies for healing. The idea of enabling the ordinary person to become effective in prayer was hugely attractive to British churches and felt like a rejection of élitism. For some it offered an alternative and corrective path to the tendencies of Restorationism, which was reaching its zenith at about the same period. There was a liberating dimension to Wimber's ministry.

A third element contributing to the impact of the movement was its shift away from the theological categories of Pentecostalism in search of more dynamic paradigms for the Spirit's work. The contested phrase "baptism of the Spirit" was gradually displaced by the more functional and flexible notion of "anointing." Gifts of the Spirit were not limited in number and not the possession of the individual, rather they were dynamically given according to situation and need. The focus was placed upon the intimacy of the believer's relationship with the Spirit who enables, rather than on proof of ownership of the gifts. For a charismatic movement still struggling to disentangle experience of God from inherited and clumsy theological descriptions of that experience, these more dynamic categories, especially when advocated by undoubtedly Spirit-filled people, served to push the movement beyond some of the dead-locked debates of earlier days. This added to the appeal of the movement to some who had been suspicious of charismatic renewal, and enabled access to it.

John Wimber's influence spread widely and he formed lasting friendships throughout many divergent church organizations. This perhaps points to a fourth element contributing to the penetration of the movement, which is to do with Wimber's own personality and style. Gentle, genial, and affable, he communicates warmth and affirmation. The laid-back, non-dogmatic pragmatism of Californian culture is well illustrated in him. However his ministry may be assessed, there is no doubt that his intention is to do good, to help people, and to treat them with respect and honor. Although immensely successful in outward terms, his frank testimonies also reveal someone well acquainted with personal pain. All of this contributes to his acceptability.

This chapter is not an attempt to give an exhaustive analysis of the signs and wonders movement. (A longer chapter would give an opportunity to examine Wimber's theological framework—especially the emphasis on the kingdom; his commitment to a pilgrimage existence which is always learning and reflecting, to personal dignity and to the whole Church of Christ in all its manifestations; his understanding of the nature of the Church and its growth; and his contributions to new and deeply personal forms of worship.) Here our attention will be given to selected areas where, in our opinion, there is the need for further reflection. We shall see that a consistent thesis is propounded, but much is left unsaid concerning the positive, and sometimes overlooked, contributions this movement has made to the contemporary scene.

We shall be approaching this task with the idea of "focus" in mind. It is unhelpful to adopt the approach of some and see Wimber as an enemy to be resisted. Rather should it be seen that all the elements to be found in the Vineyard movement have their rightful place in the landscape of Christian thought and experience. As so often, the concern has really to do with the focus that is given to those individual elements within the context of the whole. Therefore, at no point shall we suggest that the signs and wonders movement is anything other than a work of God. We shall, however, seek to reflect upon how that work is to be understood and where the focus should be given. In doing this we are also conscious of the fact that these same questions are being posed from within the movement itself. We are thus engaged not so much in a one-sided critique as in a continuing dialogue.

The Question of Dualism[2]

Like all parts of the charismatic movement, the signs and wonders movement has a tendency to a heightened dualism. I mean by this the high profile given to the ideas of Satan and spiritual warfare. The motif of a conflict between two kingdoms, good and evil, is of course thoroughly biblical, and yet we shall argue that if over-pressed it has the capacity to "eat up" or obscure other dimensions of theology and experience in an unhelpful way. We choose to begin in this area not because it is the most serious, but because it enables us to introduce a theme that will emerge consistently throughout this whole chapter, the theme of "the natural."

John Wimber comes close to an unwholesome dualism by suggesting that the earth is Satan's territory rather than the Lord's, by reading biblical texts as though they are references to Satan when this is not necessary, and by eclipsing from our view the realm of the natural. An example of this tendency would be his treatment of Jesus' rebuking of the sea in Mark 4:35–41. Because Jesus says "be muzzled," Wimber concludes that He is rebuking the "demon of the seas."[3] Similarly, because Jesus rebukes the fever suffered by Peter's mother-in-law, Wimber concludes that its cause was a demon and that "Jesus frequently spoke the same way to fevers as He did to demons, *because He saw an integral unity between sickness and Satan.*"[4] The implication of this statement should not go unnoticed, since it contributes to the high profile given to healing in the movement. Because of the identity of sickness with Satan, the motif of spiritual warfare must be applied. Sickness is no more acceptable than is the devil. Likewise, because Christ came to destroy the work of the devil and gave His disciples authority over it, they must relentlessly oppose it on every front. This does not mean for Wimber that every sickness is specifically caused by a demon.[5] He distinguishes between those who are sick and demonized and those who are "just sick."[6] But in a less direct sense there is seemingly "an integral unity between sickness and Satan."

My concern here is that this puts things out of focus. There is no need to deny the possibility that some sickness may have a demonic cause, but do we need to see all sickness as in integral unity with Satan and therefore calling forth only uncompromising hostility? On this view, to remain unhealed is in some way still to be the victim of the evil one. There is little room here for peaceful resignation and acceptance. This was graphically illustrated by the comment made by Blaine Cook, a Wimber lieutenant, on BBC Radio after the death of David Watson, a close friend of John Wimber: "Satan murdered David Watson." David was apparently a casualty in the war between the kingdoms of light and darkness.[7] I hold this to be a heightened dualism, an overstatement of the case.

What is swallowed up in such a dualism is not so much the vision of God's power, but what I am going to call in the theme which will emerge persistently, "the natural." A heightened dualism resolves the whole of reality into God and Satan, good and evil, and eclipses the realm of the natural, so depriving us of a category essential for the full understanding of human beings. This is nicely illustrated in one booklet on the subject, which, having pointed out Wimber's tendency to dualism, then goes on to ask: "Is it possible to have a cold in peace without it being a spiritual issue?"[8]

To see sickness in terms of "the natural" changes our attitude to it. There are extensive areas of created reality, of creatureliness, that need to be explored before we come anywhere near understanding our existence. These areas are often bypassed in some traditions of theology, and we are the poorer for this. This is not to imply that sickness is necessarily natural in that it belongs to the structure of God's world. Nor is it to deny that the function of sickness, personally and socially, can be such as to imprison people, leading to the need for them to be delivered. But much if not most sickness can best be understood as the consequence of the world's disorder and alienation arising out of resistance to God. Sickness is distressing and even tragic, and is legitimately the object of the Church's healing ministry; but to accept it as part of the disorder of nature in a world resistant to God, even as we accept death, may also be a dignifying and liberating experience. This option is hardly open to us if we insist on perpetually identifying Satan and sickness. We can then only ever remain radically unreconciled to it. A heightened dualism puts things out of focus. In relation to sickness, a clearer focus is gained when it is viewed as the consequence of disorder in the natural realm.

Understanding Healing

We have already touched upon the central importance given to the healing ministry, and especially to miraculous healing, in the signs and wonders movement. It is believed to be in keeping with the evangelistic methods of the early church that the presence of the kingdom of God is awakened through dramatic acts of power signaling the redeeming presence of God. Learning to heal, and not only to pray for healing, is a crucial issue and is given a prominent focus. This is in keeping with the logic that so closely identifies sickness and Satan. To advance the kingdom must also mean to heal the sick. As a claim, this is clear enough. Yet there remain confusions in John Wimber's teaching in this realm.

For instance, there are inconsistencies in the testimony to healing. Sometimes the impression is given that Vineyard churches are consistently seeing miraculous healings, at other times that they struggle in this area with little result. An example of the former is the often-quoted and astounding statement: "Today we see hundreds of people healed every month in Vineyard Christian Fellowship services. Many more are healed as we pray for them in hospitals, on the streets, and in homes. The blind see; the lame walk; the deaf hear. Cancer is disappearing!"[9] Over against this is the research by Dr. David Lewis that suggests that at a Vineyard conference only 32% of those who received prayer reported a high level of healing after the event. (Even these figures need to be read with Lewis's own remarks concerning subjective interpretations of healing in mind.[10]) At the other end of the spectrum is the reported conversation in Australia in which Wimber acknowledged that in the case of praying for children with Down's syndrome, only one out of two hundred children prayed for showed any signs of healing.

This turns out to be less than that achieved by the health-care professionals.[11]

The actual facts about the extent of healing as opposed to the claims made about it are exceedingly difficult to determine. We cannot help but feel, with others, that the vast majority of claimed healings are in the area of the placebo effect. It must, of course, be conceded that just as sickness is complex, so is healing. A changed attitude to sickness is itself a form of healing. But it does not appear to be the case that there is much evidence for miraculous healing taking place such as we see in the ministry of Jesus and such as can be called "signs of the kingdom." The rhetoric about miraculous healing far exceeds the reality. The testimonies to healing do not appear to be of the same order as the miracles of the New Testament. And this, in itself, assumes that the importance of the healing miracles of Jesus consists in the extent to which the natural order was overturned by acts of power. It is far more accurate to see that the "sign" value of the works of Jesus was more to do with whom He was healing than with what He was healing them from. The objects of Jesus' compassion were normally the rejected, the helpless, the despised, and the excluded. The effect of healing them was to allow them to reenter the worshiping community of Israel. It is difficult to see how this element is maintained when healing is being practiced upon already wealthy and privileged Westerners.

In addition to confusion concerning the evidence for actual healing, there are signs of inconsistencies in the theology of healing that John Wimber is espousing. On the one hand there are statements that imply God's universal will to heal; on the other there are those that suggest that His will to heal is selective. For instance:

> Causes of disease may be physical, psychological, spiritual. Regardless of the cause, though, Christians have power over disease. Christians in the first century saw disease as a work of Satan, a weapon of his demons, a way in which evil rules the world. When Jesus healed disease, whether demonically or physically caused, he pushed back the kingdom of Satan. There was nothing the devil did that Jesus did not undo.[12]

In contrast, on other occasions Wimber stresses the selectiveness of God's healing.[13] He points out, for instance, that when Jesus went to the Pool of Bethesda, He healed only one among the whole crowd of sick people who were there; and he frequently uses the idea that we can only do what the Father is doing. Between these two affirmations concerning a universal and selective will-to-heal there is a plain tension that is nowhere resolved. Indeed, Wimber appears to slip from one approach to the other according to the needs of the argument. It is important to focus these options more fully since they are bound to determine practice.

The logic that affirms the universal will-to-heal is compelling. Jesus healed the sick (Mark 1:34), He gave such authority to His disciples (Luke 9:1), and He commanded them to heal the sick (Luke 10:8; Matthew 10:8).[14] The clear conclusion is that "God wants to heal the sick today. It is God's nature to heal people and he has called us to reflect his nature."[15] Yet divine healing becomes effective only where there is faith. This is not necessarily the faith of the person being prayed for, but could be that of those surrounding them.[16] Wimber is anxious to avoid the pastorally damaging conclusion that those who are unhealed are therefore lacking in faith. He points out: "In the New Testament only those who pray for others' healing are berated for their lack of faith; the sick person is never chastised for lack of faith."[17]

The lines of the argument are lucid. God is a healing God, and it is only unbelief that stops Him from doing miracles. The dangers of this approach have been well rehearsed. In speaking of healing in these terms, it awakens the expectation of healing, which all too often is dashed when it does not in fact occur. The expectation is increased when healers "speak healing" (part of the Wimber methodology) into an individual and command symptoms and afflictions to abate, and even more so when a person is singled out by a "word of knowledge." It is beyond doubt that this approach arouses greater expectations than are actually fulfilled. This is the problem with Wimber's otherwise admirable statement: "I decided long ago that if I pray for one hundred people and only one is healed, it is better than if I never pray at all and no one is healed."[18] Typically, Wimber seeks to come to terms with those who are not healed by arguing that sometimes God overcomes evil by accomplishing His purpose through it even though His will is to heal.[19]

A criticism sometimes made of Wimber is that he has a defective view of divine sovereignty and that consequently anyone suffering from physical illness is taught only to be satisfied with physical healing instead of seeing God's will worked out in their pain.[20] In fact, as we have seen, Wimber does also seek to encompass this sense of the sovereignty of God without denying the position already outlined. He refers (somewhat uncommittedly) to the possibility that God is selective in whom He heals, and he draws on the work of Colin Brown to the effect that God gives no specific promise to heal. There is, he says, a difference between forgiveness and healing, since when God forgives it is a "covenanted mercy," but when He heals it is an "uncovenanted mercy."[21] In plain language, this means that forgiveness is guaranteed where there is the faith to receive it, but healing is never guaranteed even where there is the faith to receive it.

This is a very different line of country from that we first explored. It also appears to contradict other reported statements. For instance, when Wimber argues that if forgiveness is preached and not all receive it because of unbelief, we nevertheless go on preaching it, and we do likewise with healing, he is in fact arguing that healing and forgiveness are parallel and dependent on the same condition. This point was picked up in an Australian interview:

> When asked if he would be open about the small probability of healing, he declined. He wants to encourage people to put their faith in God and call upon him for healing. He wants people to know that God can heal and wants to heal and therefore to ask expectantly. He paralleled this to salvation/forgiveness. He said that we do not say to people that they only have a chance of being saved. We say that God can save and wants to save and so we encourage people to put their faith in God and call for forgiveness. Such a confusion of categories is appalling.[22]

It seems beyond doubt that Wimber is guilty of contradiction. One suspects that this is in part owing to the fact that he relies, both for his theological research and for his writing, upon assistants, and may not have fully digested what has been written in his name. All of Wimber's books are co-authored with Kevin Springer, and this is publicly acknowledged in the title pages of his books. Nevertheless, it comes as a surprise to read in the Australian publication *John Wimber: Friend or*

Foe? the astonishing statement: "John Wimber explained that his book [*Power Evangelism*] was not written by him, but came from tapes and notes of his seminars. He had not read the manuscript in detail or critically before its publication."[23] There is reason to believe that some of what has been written in his name does not represent the way he thinks, and specifically that the train of thought concerning "uncovenanted mercies" is not natural to him. My conclusion is that contradictory statements are being made about the scope of God's healing intention. On the one hand an all but universal offer of healing is made, to be limited only by human unbelief. On the other, non-healing is explained in part by references to the sovereign freedom of God.

However, before thinking too badly of Wimber's theology, it is as well to remember that it is not unknown in the theological enterprise to affirm mutually contradictory and paradoxical statements. This is most obviously so in the Calvinist-Arminian debates concerning the scope of God's saving intention. There is at several points of Christian theology a tension between universalism and particularism. We should hesitate before accusing Wimber and his associates of theological naiveté.

A Possible Reconstruction

The conundrum which Wimber inadvertently poses is not peculiar to his own contribution. We often hit up against it in the mystery of healing and in wider reflection on God's saving activity. One way to resolve it would be to argue clearly for the selective will-to-heal approach and escape into the mystery of divine sovereignty. On a previous occasion I attempted to penetrate the mystery by arguing that the command to heal was a limited command given to the disciples for the mission to Israel alone.[24] Further reflection leads me to believe that this is inadequate and that it is indeed necessary to see God's saving and healing love in universal terms.

To extend this argument, it is helpful to refer to a criticism of Wimber by J. I. Packer, who is among those who argue that Wimber's view of the sovereignty of God is defective:

> My God is not frustrated by any failure on man's part (as

Wimber suggests). I think that is the Bible's view of God: He is a sovereign God; He does whatever He pleases ... God works out all things according to His own will (Ephesians 1:11). God does whatever He pleases (Psalm 135). And if you are going to lose sight of that aspect of the matter, well then, your doctrine of God is out of shape.[25]

This leads to the accusation by others that Wimber is guilty of "radical Arminianism," that is, he stresses human ability to believe and God's inability to act where there is not faith. The view that God often does not get His way in the world and is regularly thwarted is regarded as a questionable doctrine of God.[26]

We certainly agree that this is the core of the matter, but are not in accord with the above criticisms. No one wishes to deny that God does what He pleases. The question is, however, what does it please God to do? What is at stake is how we conceive of the will of God and the way He exercises His sovereignty. Does God fulfil His sovereign purpose by overbearingly imposing His will, or by graciously bearing and enduring rejection by His creation in such a way as to overcome that resistance and to fulfil His will through and beyond it? The God who is revealed in the story of Israel, and supremely in the cross of Christ, is the God who brings human beings into partnership with himself, seeking their response and cooperation. He gives them that ability to contradict and resist Him (surely the essence of sin), and this means that in the short term His will can indeed be thwarted. The divine sovereignty does not mean the continual imposition of God's will, but that in the fullness of time God's will and purpose will be accomplished as His love overcomes our opposition to it. This is entirely consistent with the revelation of God in Christ, and if it is regarded as a doctrine out of shape, we need to question where our ideas of God come from.

It is possible and necessary to argue that the love of God goes out to all creation, seeking to save and to heal. What hinders the love of God fulfilling its purpose is the resistance that it meets. Yet we encountered before the simple fact that even where there is response to God, not all those who have genuine faith—indeed only a small minority—are healed in any way that could be called "miraculous." If we take the line that this is due to human fault, to sin and unbelief, we run once more the grave danger of pushing the sick even further into the dust. Is there, then, another way of understanding the human resistance to God which puts the matter in another light?

Here we take up once more the concept of "the natural." Human existence, and nature with it, are in disorder. No individual stands alone, but each is part of a matrix of personal, social, and environmental relationships that hold them fast. Individuals may be responsive to God on their own account, but none is fully free to experience the fullness of salvation and healing until not only they but nature itself, the sphere of created reality, is healed. It is for this reason that, although salvation may be real in the here and now, it is never complete until all creation is transformed into the new heaven and earth in which righteousness dwells. Jürgen Moltmann makes this point in slightly different language:

> There are also objective unjust circumstances which make people ill, as social medicine has shown. So it is often impossible to heal the sick without healing their relationships, the circumstances in which they live, and the social structures of the social system to which they belong ... It therefore makes sense not to consider diseases solely in the isolation of their pathogenic causes, but to see those who are ill in the context of their life history, and to view their life history as part of their social history.[27]

So it is possible to conceive of why it is that healing does not come to people until all the factors which make for their sickness are transcended in the new creation. In saying this we illuminate not just the fact that the kingdom is "now and not yet," but also why this is the case. The kingdom is not yet fully here because there is still resistance to it within the sphere of the created, supremely in human beings, who are the key elements within the natural sphere, and in the societies and cultures that arise from their existence. To make this statement does not, however, remove all mystery, for the mystery remains concerning why it is that the healing God freely chooses on some occasions to overcome the barriers of human resistance and to manifest His glory. An approach that takes seriously the ability of humans to resist God must also take seriously His grace and persistence in overcoming that resistance and must acknowledge that how God acts in His freedom is His decision and not our own. We do not in this reconstruction eliminate all mystery, but we do see that God's particular acts of mercy are to be placed within an understanding of His universal saving outreach to an undeserving world. To reckon with the category of the natural enables us to maintain a clearer focus.

Spiritual Phenomena

A third area for investigation concerns those phenomena already described that accompany John Wimber's ministry. Unusual though these are, there is biblical and historical testimony to the fact that when God draws near, the effect upon the human system can be overpowering. The category of "the natural" enables us to assert that these phenomena are essentially varied human responses to the approach of the transcendent God. As such they should not be over-valued. If they are seen as the direct workings of God, such that He deliberately makes persons tremble or laugh uproariously or weep, we are left with the question why He does these things to some and not to others, and are led to the possible but faulty conclusion that absence of phenomena means absence of divine activity. More seriously, we might make superficial judgments about the work of God based upon the occurrence of the dramatic rather than on the evidence of a holy life. It is far more accurate to say that different individuals will respond to the divine in very varied ways and that there is little or no spiritual significance in the exact manner of their response.

There is more to being human than we imagine. Human consciousness is the tip of the iceberg. Nine-tenths of what we are is hidden from view and from ourselves. Each individual's spiritual experience will reflect the shape of their own make-up. The physiology of the human body, the constitution of the brain, the individual's psychology, will all be ingredients in the religious experiences that we have. To say this is by no means to reduce the significance of our experiences, but simply to describe what is taking place when there is encounter with God. To describe what is happening to someone when they are undergoing conversion, for example, does not explain the mystery of the experience. It simply elucidates what is taking place. In so doing we are developing the category of "the natural" and showing how experience of God makes its impact upon our being.

There is nothing particularly novel in what I have said in this section so far, but I wish to extend the analysis to a further area which I choose to call "the psychic," by which I mean the deep unconscious. Religious phenomena are also determined by psychic responses, and at this level some people are more responsive (we might also say more vulnerable) than others. The story of King Saul is instructive in this regard. Several times unusual psychic phenomena are recorded of him, including being caught up into ecstasy as he encounters a prophetic band (1 Samuel 10:5–6, 9–11), "burning with anger," as the Spirit of the Lord comes on him (1 Samuel 11:6), and lying all night naked prophesying at Naioth (1 Samuel 19:18–24). The way these incidents are described suggests that Saul's responses are autonomic and beyond his direct control, and it is clearly indicated that they take place even when he is backslidden. Saul's subsequent history, his manic-depression, and the desperation with which he consults the medium at Endor, all contribute to the picture of a psychically vulnerable person.

A further factor may be noted here. Saul's experiences are not simply individual. They are triggered in the first instance by a group that is caught up in prophesying. This suggests that there is a corporate dimension to the experience, subconsciously communicable within or from a group. In considering Saul's experience, we are seeing something that approximates the psychological analysis of Carl Jung, which allows for the depths within the individual but sees that at these levels we begin to merge progressively with our immediate social, then ethnic, and finally racial groupings. None of us is an island entirely unto our-selves. We are all part of the mainland.

On the basis of this analysis, it is possible to make certain descriptive statements about the Wimber phenomena. The description ought then to enable us to evaluate religious phenomena in general. I wish to argue that in the Wimber movement at least two streams of social and psychic experience have come together. One derives from the Quaker tradition and the flow of religious experience into which Wimber entered upon conversion. The more dominant stream, however, derives from the Jesus Movement of the 60s, and was decisively introduced into Wimber's experience through Lonnie Frisbee, the individual through whom Wim-ber and his church first experienced a dramatic visitation of the Spirit, and previously a leading figure in the Jesus Movement.[28] A full understanding of the Wimber movement would necessitate a detailed examination of Frisbee's antecedents. My guess is that he was the trigger for the communication of psychic phenomena in the Wimber movement of which that movement has now become the bearer. This clarifies why it is that wherever Vineyard teams go (and the use of teams is significant in this regard) they bear with them and catalyze in others the religious phenomena we are discussing. Conversely, when they depart, such phenomena recede or atrophy, depending on the degree to which any group has been formed at the psychic level by the Vineyard.

None of this analysis is meant to devalue the reality of spiritual experience in general or of the Vineyard in particular. The psychic dimension I have described is part of "the natural" and, therefore, of creation. Wherever there is experience of God, the human response will necessarily contain this element. For as long as the psychic is integrated with the spiritual it is healthy and productive in the expression of individual and corporate spirituality. However, when it is not thus integrated there may be religious phenomena which have no spiritual value and which may even become destructive. The production of religious phenomena, as in the case of Saul, is not necessarily an indicator of spirituality. Here true discernment is needed in the channeling of religious experience. Psychic or religious phenomena may become divorced or dislocated from the Spirit of God. Once triggered into life, they are apt to assume a life of their own and become self-generating. This may lead to stereotyped ritual behavior or to psychic manipulation by the unscrupulous. The pitfalls of the phenomena need to be recognized.

Conclusion

My argument has been that in evaluating the signs and wonders movement the category of "the natural" is necessary if we are to judge it rightly. To say that the movement has a reduced understanding of creation, of the natural depths that belong to the life God has given us and of the role they play in any experience of God or understanding of His work, is not to single out this movement alone as faulty at this point. This same tendency belongs to the charismatic movement as a whole, and indeed to the whole tradition of Western theology, where the tendency has been toward the neglect of nature. The dualisms that resolve reality into good and evil, God and the devil, spirit versus body, redemption versus creation, and which have despised God's creation in the name of God himself, have not served us well and need now to be transcended. The weakness of the signs and wonders movement at this point is ultimately the weakness of us all. A wider and deeper perspective would make us more discerning and more genuinely human.

Most of this chapter has been descriptive, and at no point has it been the intention to do other than reflect further on important issues raised by the Wimber movement. In his recent biography of C. S. Lewis, A. N. Wilson writes: "This book is not intended to be iconoclastic, but I will try to be realistic, not only because reality is more interesting than fantasy, but also because we do Lewis no honor to make him into a plaster saint. And he deserves our honor." A similar intention, suitably transposed to another subject, has guided us as we have attempted this analysis.

Three

Demonology and the Charismatic Movement

ANDREW WALKER

Introduction

C. S. Lewis said at the beginning of *The Screwtape Letters*:

> There are two equal and opposite errors into which our race
> can fall about the devils. One is to disbelieve in their existence.
> The other is to believe, and to feel an excessive and unhealthy
> interest in them. They themselves are equally pleased by both errors
> and hail a materialist or a magician with the same delight.[1]

For Christians to disbelieve in demons, and *ipso facto* the devil, is in
my view mistaken. Philosophically, it can lead to that sort of monism
where God is held responsible for all the suffering and evil in the world
as well as all the good. If God were truly the author of evil and confusion
as well as order and harmony, it would be legitimate to wonder whether
He is not a God of love but a cosmic sadist.

Admittedly, such a monism is more sophisticated and, I think, ultimately more defendable than a metaphysical dualism such as Persian
Zoroastrianism, which posits that there are two Gods of the universe,
the good one, and the evil one. If we were to adopt this model and make
the Christian devil equal to God, then, of course, there could be no

certainty as to the outcome of their eternal opposition. It might also seem that the devil could wield his power to destroy Christians' lives, as witnessed by Blaine Cook's now infamous remark that the devil murdered Canon David Watson.[2]

However, unless one is prepared to override the biblical witness, it is difficult to reject completely the devil and the notion of a spiritual war between the forces of good and evil. Again, I believe that in this matter Lewis is right:

> Real Christianity (as distinct from Christianity-and-water) goes much nearer to Dualism than people think. One of the things that surprised me when I first read the New Testament seriously was that it was always talking about a Dark Power in the universe—a mighty evil spirit who was held to be the Power behind death and disease, and sin. The difference is that Christianity thinks this Dark Power was created by God, and was good when he was created, and went wrong. Christianity agrees with Dualism that his universe is at war. But it doesn't think this is a war between independent powers. It thinks it's a civil war, a rebellion, and that we are living in a part of the universe occupied by the rebel.[3]

This sense of drama and conflict is not only typical of Lewis—we remember how he uses it to good effect in *The Lion, the Witch, and the Wardrobe*[4]—but it also echoes what Gustav Aulen called, in his book *Christus Victor*,[5] "the classical model of atonement." This patristic model draws heavily on the sense of battle or spiritual warfare between God and the devil. The church fathers seemed quite at home with the mythological and conflict language of angels and demons. Perhaps we recall the eighth-century hymn of St. Andrew of Crete which we sing each Advent:

> Christian doest thou see them on the holy ground,
> How the hosts of darkness compass thee around?
> Christian, up and smite them, counting gain but loss:
> Smite them, Christ is with thee, soldier of the cross.[6]

This sort of talk infuriated the liberal theologians of the nineteenth century, for they thought it crude and pre-scientific, but I think the Fathers had grasped a central fact of the Atonement which later and more rational theories obscured. That fact is that God's work on the cross included not only the overcoming of death and the ending of enmity between himself and humankind, but also the defeat of the devil. There is strong scriptural warrant for such a view: "Now is the time for judgment on this world; now the prince of this world will be driven out. But I, when I am lifted up from the earth, will draw all men to myself" (John 12:31–32); and again, "The reason the Son of God appeared was to destroy the devil's work" (1 John 3:8).

However, it is precisely at this point that my problems begin. For having sided with Lewis against the liberal and modernist position that there is no devil, and therefore no Christian dualism of any kind, I find myself recoiling from much of the literature, tape ministries, and theology that some modern-day charismatics promote under the broad rubric of "spiritual warfare."

The Paranoid Universe

Psychologically speaking, paranoia is that mental state in which we find ourselves abnormally mistrusting and suspecting others. Paranoid people typically see themselves as persecuted by their enemies, and they see their enemies everywhere. In psychotic case-studies enemies range from communists—or capitalists—to extra-terrestrial beings, including demonic angels. Sometimes an extreme sense of persecution is matched by delusions of grandeur, whereby those who are deluded have special powers or attributes which alone can save themselves and others from the evils that will destroy the world.[7]

Paranoia need not only be understood as a medical condition of individuals, for it is catching and can so easily become a group phenomenon. If such groups become dominated by a paranoid world view that militates against rational and common-sense interpretations of reality, then clearly there is trouble in store. Such groups have a tendency to physical or social isolation where there is little chance that critical and sensible ways of dealing with things will prevail. Obviously Jonestown in Guyana would be the paradigm of extreme psycho-social paranoia, but cults, sects, holy huddles, self-selected elite groups, even the "in-crowd," are in danger of becoming both the perpetrators and the victims of a paranoid universe.

A belief in the devil and demonic powers does not in itself entail paranoia, either in the strict medical sense or as a social neurosis. In the third-century writings of St. Anthony of Egypt, for example, we see ample evidence of a belief in demons, but hardly a blind terror of them. Indeed, stemming from St. Anthony, and becoming normative in the Christian East throughout the Middle Ages, a sound psychology of the spiritual life developed that distinguished between God's acts, the devil's ploys, and the normal processes of the natural world. The fallen and natural world included the human will, neither yet demonized nor yet redeemed. The Fathers' insistence that we must discern fallen but natural forces from intrinsically evil ones is one of the great bequests of the patristic era to Christianity.

A Christian world view that is divided into the tripartite arenas of the divine, the natural, and the demonic is unlikely to fall prey to a paranoia that dissects the world into "us" and "them." Charismatic theologies and methodologies that do tend to divide the cosmos into God's kingdom of light and Satan's kingdom of darkness are in constant danger of first adopting a paranoid world view, and then becoming entrapped and socialized into the paranoid universe.

Throughout the history of Christianity, if we allow for certain exceptional periods of paranoia—e.g., heretics and the Inquisition during the waning of the Middle Ages, and witchcraft and the Salem witch-hunts—we will find that beliefs in demons and efficacy of exorcisms rarely gets out of hand. It is true that occasionally hysteria ran rife in monasteries, as one would expect in such socially isolated institutions. And sometimes Christian beliefs in the supernatural world would be adulterated by folk-superstitions such as the evil eye. But on the whole the devil and his works were kept in their place: powerful, yes, but never dominant, and never center stage.

Even today many Catholic, Anglican, and Orthodox traditionalists would agree with the report of the Bishop of Exeter on exorcism in 1972,[8] that demonism is a reality, but is nonetheless rare.

This is in fact my own view—though it is one which, admittedly, satisfies neither a modernist nor a certain kind of fundamentalist. And at this point it is time to ask: When did that kind of fundamentalism arise whereby demons began to break loose from the subterranean moorings of the unconscious and surface in open rebellion with the fury of what the house-church leader Dave Tomlinson has called "char-ismania"?

One answer might be: "With the birth of the Pentecostal Movement at the turn of the century." Now it is true that classical Pentecostalism is primarily dualistic and initially had little room for the natural world, even as a buffer or no-man's-land between the kingdoms of darkness and light. But it is a matter of empirical record that Pentecostalism has not been overcome by demonic infestations. On the contrary, and not-withstanding the influence in the 1920s of Jessie Penn-Lewis's blood-curdling book *War on the Saints,*[9] denominations such as Elim and the Assemblies of God have believed in demons but have kept them firmly under the bed and firmly under control. There has been little interest or fascination in the habits, habitat or *haute couture* of evil spirits.

I think there are three reasons why, historically, classical Pentecos-talism did not capitulate to paranoia. First, unlike much of the charis-matic renewal movement, it was essentially evangelistic in nature: its revivalistic impulse was heaven-bent on saving souls. Its evangelism therefore kept it outward-looking and Christ-centered, leaving its de-monism in the wake of its excitement and enthusiasm. It was there, all right, but it was peripheral and virtually out of sight. Second, Pente-costalists were too entranced with their own Pentecost—with its tongues, healings, and singalong songs—to be bewitched by beguiling theories of demonism. And third, Pentecostalists may have been edu-cationally disadvantaged, but they were not stupid. What they lacked in cultural finesse they made up with working-class common sense.

To ask when the paranoid universe came into being is, in fact, to ask for nothing less than a major historical investigation. That work still remains to be done, but let me suggest one line of inquiry which may be worth pursuing.

I think the origins may lie in the late 1940s and 1950s, in the North American movement known as the "Latter Day Rain." It was the time of William Branham, a man who talked with angels, argued with de-mons, and diagnosed illnesses through the colors of the aura. Two young men associated with him at that time were Ern Baxter, who was later to become a major figure in the so-called "shepherding" or discipleship movement, and Paul Cain, a prophet from a Pentecostal Holiness background who until recently was associated with the Kansas City prophets and the ministry of John Wimber.

Other itinerant charismatics not directly associated with the movement also began to make their mark in the 1950s. Oral Roberts, who was also from the holiness tradition of Pentecostalism, pioneered "slaying in the Spirit" in his tent meetings (though this phenomenon is most closely associated with two women, Maria Woodworth-Etter and Kathryn Kuhlman). Like Branham, Roberts would claim that disease in the sick person's body caused his praying hand to swell and extend. Roberts came from Oklahoma, which has also produced two other controversial Pentecostalists—T. L. Osborn and Kenneth Hagin.[10]

A. A. Allen was the most extravagant maverick of the 1950s and early 1960s. His most infamous claim probably being that on one occasion following prayer God turned dentist and supernaturally filled a man's teeth. And yet on demonic matters he bears a close resemblance to the Latter Day Rain movement. He wrote copiously on demonic oppression and possession, and pioneered tape ministries in which he purported to talk with evil spirits. It became fashionable in his churches to talk to the spirits of lust, anger, and jealousy. Years later this sort of talk became so established in some charismatic circles that Frank and Ida Mae Hammond could talk of "the spirit of nervousness" and the "demon of heart attack." Allen, it was reported, even talked of the "spirit of nicotine." I am not certain whether he liberalized that old expression "the demon drink," but I do know that he died a hopeless alcoholic in a hotel room in San Francisco.

We could trace the influence of Allen, Hagin, and Roberts on modern charismatics, but I think a more profitable line to follow would be to show the personal and theological link between Branham, Baxter, and the group known as "The Fort Lauderdale 5"; we might even, using language similar to Nigel Wright's, talk of a "psychic trace."

Two members of this group, Don Basham and Derek Prince, not only majored on shepherding and, along with the others, peddled strong views on male leadership, but in the 1970s they also pioneered a belief in the prevalence of witchcraft in our societies and in the danger of amulets and charms, which they saw as demonically infused, or at least under the dominance of Satan. They talked not only of demons as disembodied spirits trying to control individual bodies, they also talked of "strong men," super-demonic powers that dominated—along with the lesser devils—churches, cities, and whole nations. Prince's work in particular was a major influence on Frank and Ida Mae Hammond and their disturbing deliverance ministry as outlined in their book *Pigs in the Parlor*.[11] There are echoes of Prince's and the Hammonds' work throughout North America and Great Britain in the 1980s. It resounded and resonated most clearly, however, in New Zealand through the self-deliverance techniques of Graham and Shirley Powell[12] and the ministry of Bill Subritzky. It is probably Subritzky, a lawyer by training, and an Anglican layman, who has had the greatest impact upon Anglican and now independent charismatic church exorcisms in Great Britain in the late 1980s and early 1990s.

It is wrong to make *ad hominem* remarks or pass moral judgments on the integrity and Christian commitment of such people as Bill Subritzky, Derek Prince, and their fellow-travelers, but I do believe that their view of the devil and his powers has helped create—unwittingly— a paranoid universe. For since the 1970s, but with gathering rapidity in the 1980s, demons began to come out from beneath the beds and, like *Gremlins 2: The New Batch*, they got out of control. Their infestation was progressive: at first charismatics tended to see demons only in the world, and thought it better to play safe and stay in the Church. Then some found that the devil would snipe at you if you left the sanctuary of radically renewed fellowships. (This was a feature of certain Restorationist churches for a while.) But then it was found that the demons could get into the sanctuary, and indeed it was really Christians who were in danger of demonization. As Frank Hammond puts it: "Does everyone need deliverance? Personally, I have not found any exceptions!"[13]

The Subritzky model also succeeds in some Christian groups precisely because its supporters believe that the demons will prey on everyone within the local church. In such a context it is difficult for the skeptical believer to oppose the charismatic leader and discerner of evil spirits, for one runs the risk of being said to be under the control of that most hated of demons, "the spirit of criticism."

In the paranoid universe, not only can Christians become demonized, but so too can whole social groups. For example, other world religions are not simply different, wrong, in error, or as Lewis would prefer to see it, unfulfilled: they are agents of devilish control. And homosexuals are not to be seen as exercising a preference, suffering from a sickness, or living in old-fashioned sin: they are under demonic thrall. It is but a short step from these positions to xenophobia, homophobia, and hate-filled persecution. How strange that the heightened experience of persecution which is the hallmark of the paranoid universe is inverted, so that fighting back at your supposed enemies entails persecuting your alleged persecutors. This is what happens when spiritual warfare becomes an attempt to match power with power, meet hate with hate of hate, rather than as Jesus commanded, "Love your enemies, do good to those who hate you, bless those who curse you, pray for those who mistreat you" (Luke 6:27–28).

In the paranoid universe women are particularly prone to persecution, especially if they are feminists. Feminism is under the province of the spirit of Jezebel, or so says Don Basham.[14] This spirit's speciality is domination, and feminism is seen as an attempt by women to switch roles with men. Women are apparently particularly prone to domination, which Derek Prince understands to be the essence of witchcraft. For Prince it is a fact that most witches are women, and what he calls the Pentecostal witch is one of the most dangerous kinds. She is the sort of woman who wants to usurp what he sees as the rightful leadership of men, or does not go along with the male headship theology.[15]

One begins to suspect that any woman who becomes critical of men, or is simply a strong personality, is a prime candidate for the dehumanizing label "demonized." This suspicion is somewhat confirmed by one of Don Basham's tapes,[16] in which he unfolds what he sees as the proper role of women and men in creation. What disturbs me about his views is that much of his understanding of female and male roles in society has little to do with the Bible or a thorough grasp of cross-cultural studies, but owes a great deal to his own amateur psychologizing, male prejudices, and somewhat inventive use of gender archetypes.

On this subject, I received a long letter from a "house church" elder in Ireland, who told me:

> Looking at the overall picture I feel that the fundamentalist line
> of theology that the Americans brought with them led us to see
> difficulties as black and white issues. This was extrapolated from

the early teaching on spiritual warfare, an unhealthy form of "du-alism," whereby God and Satan are constantly warring over every trivial issue in our lives. Personal choice and responsibility for our lives seems to be only interpreted in terms of siding with God through an overly superstitious view of "guidance."

He then went on to tell me of the effect that one of Prince's tapes on women and witchcraft had had on the church. Suddenly, he said, men everywhere began to see their wives demonized and in need of deliv-erance. There was a spirit of fear and suspicion abroad that caused real division within the fellowship.

And it is here that we move to the heart of the problem. Paranoia breeds fear. Ironically, what is demonic about the paranoid universe is not that it is a world that suddenly sees demons everywhere, but that it is a world in bondage to fear. As evangelist Geoff Crocker reminded me, the Scriptures tell us that "perfect love casts out fear" (1 John 4:18), and yet we find that fellowships that see demons everywhere first become fearful, and out of their fear they then become belligerent.

We see what amounts to a fascinated fearfulness in the dramatic details of how demons enter human beings. And it would seem that they can enter any way they choose: through abortion, sexual inter-course, the womb during pregnancy, a traumatic birth, genetic inheri-tance. Subritzky tells us:

> I prayed with a man, aged 40, who had a spirit of abortion in him and he curled up like a fetus and screamed. As others minis-tered with me, we saw this man totally delivered. His mother had tried to abort him while he was in the womb, hence the spirit of abortion had entered him.[17]

Again he tells us:

> When sexual intercourse takes place outside of marriage, strong spirits or demons of lust and perverted sex can pass from one body to another during the act of sexual intercourse.[18]

Subritzky is never short of shock-horror revelation: he tells us that "On many occasions, demons enter during pregnancy or at birth. De-mons can easily enter a fetus where there is shock, fear or trauma on the part of the mother, particularly where there is disagreement between the parents."[19] Apparently demons do not always succeed in penetration or infusion: sometimes they just cling on. Subritzky explains that, "It is interesting to note that the Bible describes Satan as Beelzebub or 'Lord of the Flies.' On occasions I have seen spirits like flies attached to the back of a person's head."[20]

The fascination with demonic entrance is matched by an equal fascination with their exit. Vomiting, spitting, foaming—Subritzky calls these the "demonic nests"—and coughing are typical pathways of expulsion. Balls of slime and alien globules have been popular from the days of A. A. Allen. Tom Smail tells us of the time he went to a Pittsburgh charismatic conference organized by Don Basham. It was decided to have a mass deliverance of the spirit of masturbation, and so kleenex were handed out to the young men (there is no mention of the women), who on the words of deliverance were to cough up the troublesome demon. Tom's reflection on this whole episode must surely be ours: he said that he did not know whether to laugh or cry. It is hard, even with charity, not to laugh when Subritzky tells us that another frequent manifestation of demons leaving is yawning. "Sometimes," he says, "these particular demons cause people to go to sleep during meetings, particularly when the gospel is being preached. Sometimes yawning is also accompanied by sighing as demons leave a person."[21]

But in the paranoid universe the demons can also reach us indirectly, especially through charms, artifacts, and bracelets. When in 1986 Derry Knight managed to extract $500,000 from well-meaning but gullible charismatic Christians, perhaps the most disturbing aspect of the whole affair was their belief that Knight could seriously dent the devil's power by destroying some old satanic regalia.

Belief in the efficacy of witchcraft and curses now seems to be mandatory in many charismatic fellowships. Demonic influence not only extends to amulets—a strong conviction of Derek Prince—but it can also invade household ornaments. Consider this cautionary tale from the Hammonds:

> While ministering to a nine-year-old girl, the mother told us
> that the girl awakened every night in the middle of the night. She

would be very frightened. They could not account for this. The ministry for the girl turned up nothing that was suspect. We asked that we might inspect the girl's bedroom. Three things were found in the room which we had discovered could attract evil spirits. There was a book about a witch—secured through the public school. Then there was a big, stuffed toy frog, and over the girl's bed was a mobile from which dangled a half dozen little owl images that glowed in the dark.

The family agreed to remove these objects and destroy them. We commanded all demons hiding in the room to leave immediately in the name of Jesus, and pled the covering of the blood of Jesus over the girl. The girl has slept peacefully ever since.[22]

They go on:

What about the owls and frogs? These are classified among the creatures mentioned in Deuteronomy 14:7–19 as being unclean and abominable. They are types of demon spirits. My ministry has taken me into many homes, and I have become aware of how many of these unclean creatures are being made into art objects and used for decorations. This especially true of owls and frogs. It is more than coincidence that both of these are creatures of darkness. They come out at night and hunt their prey. Demons are also creatures of darkness. They cannot operate in the light.[23]

So often we find that paranoia generates its own logic and quirky methods of exegesis. Who says that demons cannot operate in the light? And talking of Deuteronomy 14:7–19, the list of unclean creatures does not actually mention frogs, though they are implied. Of greater significance is the fact that the list of unclean creatures clearly refers to the strict dietary laws of the Israelites and has nothing to do with intrinsically evil beings.

It is time for us to leave the paranoid universe, but before we do, let us leave it with this thought. Paranoid beliefs breed a basic insecurity that is always looking for the men and women of power to show us the way to protect ourselves from danger. After all, a Dungeons and Dragons world, as all modern children know, needs a dungeon-master. Consequently, we should not be surprised that if we live in the paranoid universe we will look for Pentecostal "strong men" with the gnosis and power—that is, the technique—to protect us and perhaps even turn us, like them, into spiritual warriors.

The Devil, Devils, and the Bible

When we turn from the paranoid universe to the Bible, we discover many strange things about the devil. The first thing we discover is that the Old Testament has very little to say about him. Second, we find that the New Testament has a far more developed—although not systematic—treatment of the Dark Power. Third, we cannot find anywhere the sort of fascination and detailed accounts of spirit visitations, possessions, and exorcisms that we find in the paranoid universe.

In fact, the word "devil," meaning destroyer (*Abaddon* in Hebrew, *Apollyon* in Greek), is not used at all in the Old Testament. The Hebrew word for adversary or accuser, *Satan*, is used, but only ten times. Six of these occur in the book of Job.

Satan appears briefly in the Psalms, more as a rhetorical device than as a figure of significance; and Zechariah 3:2, where we read, "The Lord rebuke you, Satan!" there is little clue as to why he is introduced into the text or what his role is supposed to be. Indeed even in the book of Job, Satan is a very curious character. He appears to have more than a nodding acquaintance with God, and it is not clear whether he does God's dirty work for Him, whether he is a sort of cosmic Job's comforter, or whether he is a nasty and irritating opponent of God who nevertheless seems in some way to be His servant or at least subservient to Him.[24]

In the New Testament things are quite different. The devil, either as *Satan* or *Apollyon/Diabolis*, is mentioned well over eighty times. Here we see the sort of dualism that Lewis discovered when he first read the New Testament carefully. The devil appears in multiple guises. He is, among other things, the angel of the pit (Revelation 9:11), the god of this world or this age (2 Corinthians 4:4), the prince of darkness (Ephesians 6:12), the prince of this world (John 12:31), and the dragon (Revelation 12:7).

And yet there is no exposition of his origins. Christ's enigmatic line, "I saw Satan fall like lightning from heaven" (Luke 10:14), is his only comment, and while it appears to echo Isaiah 14:12, "How you are fallen from heaven, O Lucifer, son of the morning," the Old Testament context would seem to suggest that a historical person is the subject of this description, not a cosmic being. Whatever the case, the New Testament, like the Old, does not fully reveal the nature of the Evil One (though Jesus does tell us that the devil was a murderer and liar from the beginning (John 8:44).

In my opinion, the unsystematic and somewhat haphazard treatment of the devil in the Bible is a signal to us not to attempt to know more. At the very least, we should take note that, in revealing fully to us the Christ, the canon of Scripture speaks of the devil only in mythological language, often in uncertain and unexplained passages, and sometimes in blunt warnings to have no dealings with him (e.g., Ephesians 4:27).

Turning to the devils, we find that they are mentioned only ten times in the Old Testament (though there are nine references to unexplained familiar spirits in the Pentateuch). Excluding the complex use of Paul's nine references to the "powers" in the New Testament, they are mentioned less than thirty times. Most of these references relate to the ministry of Jesus in the Synoptic Gospels (e.g., Matthew 4:24; Mark 5:12).

It is the ministry of Jesus that provides the clearest New Testament data for the subject of demonism and exorcism. Some charismatics see such material as providing not merely case studies but inalienable proof texts, because they take it that Jesus as God could not have been mistaken in His spiritual discernment. We might counter such a view on the grounds that such a Christology does not leave room for the full humanity of Christ. To say with the universal Church that our Lord never sinned is not the same thing as saying that He knew all things (about sickness, for example) or never made an inaccurate statement. The patristic case for the true divinity of Christ, we should remind ourselves, did not rest on a docetic denial of a free and fallible human will; though, to use the jargon, there was no question that Jesus was gnomically deficient.

We can sidestep these arguments here, for the point at issue is not whether demonization occurs—I affirm its possibility at the beginning of this chapter—but whether the New Testament, in believing in demons, is wedded to a paranoid universe. Here the ministry of Jesus is unequivocal: He clearly believes in demons but does not see all sickness and evil under devilish control, and He shows no interest whatever in the minutiae and mechanisms of the demonic realm.

This lack of fascination with the demonic, which is the proper antidote to paranoia, is also reflected in the Acts of the Apostles. There are less than ten demonic incidents and allusions in the Lukan apostolic narratives. Similarly, Paul in his epistles has virtually nothing to say about devils, though he warns against worshiping idols and their relationship to the fellowship of demons (1 Corinthians 10:20).

Although Jesus tells us that eternal fire awaits the devil and his angels (Matthew 25:41), the origins of devils are barely mentioned anywhere in the Bible. There is of course the war in heaven of Revelation 12:7–9, but it is not without irony that many fundamentalist Bible scholars who tend to interpret Revelation as futuristic have no problem in reading this event retrospectively. Indeed the case for an angelic fall is more a matter of logical necessity, or of its value as a theological hypothesis to help explain suffering and the problem of evil, rather than one with strong biblical warrant (incidentally, a view shared by C. S. Lewis and Evelyn Underhill).

Ezekiel 28:1–17 and Isaiah 14:12–21 are sometimes cited as support for a cosmic fall, but the texts would seem to point to self-exalted human beings rather than angelic ones. At the very least, when Jesus alludes to Isaiah in His description of the fall of Satan He has backing from the Old Testament; but when Jude in his letter talks of the "angels who did not keep their proper domain" (v. 6), he would seem to cross-reference to Peter's epistle (2 Peter 2:4), but without any other canonical foundation. Indeed, when in verse 9 he talks of Michael contending with the devil, or mentions the prophecies of Enoch in verse 14 he most clearly is not drawing from the canonical tradition, but is borrowing directly from the intertestamental literature.

Despite these cautionary remarks, I think overall there is enough biblical evidence to support a proper Christian dualism, but it seems to me wise to make modest claims about the origins of devils, the working of the demonic world, and the methodology of exorcisms when the Bible remains virtually silent on these matters. Or at least, if we do speculate about them, we should call our speculations what they really are: not revelations or biblical truths, but daring thoughts which, like those elaborate Chinese kites, we hope will catch the wind and take flight.

It is in this realm of speculative kite-flying that Prince and Subritzky, among many others, do strange things to the biblical text, and are able to create not only a topography of hell, but also a fairly detailed plan of the tactics, weapons, and personalities of evil spirits. Let us take one major example. St. Paul, as I have already mentioned, makes nine references to "powers" in the New Testament. Sometimes these are without any evil connotations, such as in Colossians 1:16, "For by him all things were created: things in heaven and on earth, visible and invisible, whether thrones or powers or rulers or authorities; all things were created by him and for him." This contrasts with Ephesians 6:12, where, in the context of putting on God's armor to resist the devil, Paul says, "For our struggle is not against flesh and blood, but against the rulers, against the authorities, against the powers of this dark world and against the spiritual forces of evil in the heavenly realms." Wesley Carr's *Angels and Principalities* and Walter Wink's *Naming the Powers*[25] demonstrate most clearly the difficulty of catching Paul's drift and interpreting his language. There seems to be deliberate ambiguity in the text, whereby we are dealing with power that is corporate and yet both incorporeal as well as corporal—invisible and visible.

For what it is worth, I have argued in my book *Enemy Territory*[26] that while not needing to deny the reality of the demonic, we need to understand the dark powers as interpenetrating the power structures of society, so that we fight evil not in the realm of fantasy or the heavenlies, but in the public world of politics and economics. Hence I have suggested that we must fight collective evil wherever it is to be found, whether this be organized crime or racism. Wherever we find the oppression of nationalities, social classes, and women, the powers are at work. The same goes for bureaucratic impersonalism, warmongering, or governmental and societal indifference to poverty and suffering.

Many charismatic specialists on the demonic world interpret Paul's powers and rulers not as negative cosmic influences, nor as social/spiritual power structures, but as superior fiends. But I find their method of biblical interpretation worrying. For example, one becomes suspicious of Subritzky's whole approach when one reads that "demons can be clearly distinguished from angels because angels have wings."[27] He deduces this fact by interpreting literally the phrase "fly swiftly" predicted of Gabriel in Daniel 9:21.

The liberalizing of parable and metaphor becomes an occupational hazard in the paranoid universe. So, for example, when Jesus says in Matthew 12:29, "How can anyone enter a strong man's house and carry off his possession unless he first ties up the strong man? Then he can rob his house," this is taken by both Prince and Subritzky to indicate that there are demonic strong men. The powers and rulers of Paul now become personified into super-devils, responsible under their general, Satan, for territories, and commanding a vast array of demonic forces. This interesting interpretation is reinforced by the Hammonds' conviction that the "Prince of Persia" spoken of in Daniel 10 is a "demonic prince." Given that Daniel, like Revelation, is written in the Jewish apocalyptic genre, with its typically lurid and symbolic language, we might wonder if the text is really capable of such an interpretation. But from the Persian reference the Hammonds tell us, "From this it is clear that there are ruling demon spirits placed by Satan over nations and cities in order to carry out his evil purposes."[28]

However, it is Subritzky who presents us with the most detailed exposition of the strong men, saying that there is in effect a counterfeit unholy trinity of the three strong men—Jezebel, the spirit of antichrist, Death, and Hell. (One wonders with what model of the Holy Trinity Subritzky is working.) But let us not get on to his ground, for there is no evidence in Scripture that the spirit of antichrist of 1 John 4:3 is meant to be a cosmic demon. There is even less evidence that it is a so-called strong man. Can one really make out a case that Jezebel, whom Subritzky links with the scarlet woman and whore of Babylon, is a superior fiend? It also takes an extraordinary imagination to take the Death and Hades of Revelation 20:13–14 and amalgamate them into a monophysite strong man of the unholy trinity.

What is most disturbing about this kind of biblical exegesis is that it rests not on sound hermeneutical principles but on what Nigel Wright in his book *The Fair Face of Evil*[29] calls "inside information"—it is no less than the unholy trinity and the lower angelic hoards who tell Subritzky their names and reveal to him their powers. Indeed, Subritzky admits that he came to realize that Death and Hell were themselves a diabolical Jesus after people became violent when he commanded the spirit Death and Hell to leave them.[30] This may strike the psychologist as bordering on self-fulfilling prophecy: one predicts that Death and Hell are strong men, and, lo, the demons confirm it. It will certainly strike theologians as unbalanced, for we cannot allow our understanding of the demonic order to be dictated to us by devils, whether real or merely figments of our imagination.

Recharacterizing the Devil and Christian Spiritual Warfare

Now it is time to conclude, and I want to end with some remarks about the Evil One, and about the nature of spiritual warfare.

It strikes me that a presupposition which underlies much charismatic understanding of the demonic is that the devil is a person, with fiendish personality and a brilliant, albeit twisted, rationality. From this it tends to follow that the hosts of hell are *a fortiori* also personal. They are the counterfeits of heaven—fallen angels, like the unfallen ones except that they are committed to evil. Thus spiritual warfare can be seen in terms of battling against a well-organized and trained army with great powers of detection and destruction.

Such a view facilitates the sort of biblical exposition that we have briefly examined. It fuels the conspiratorial view of the devil that is so essential for the successful maintenance of a paranoid universe: for demons are more fearsome if one knows that they are everywhere, plotting to get us. It also helps facilitate novels such as Frank Peretti's *This Present Darkness*,[31] which while being a work of fiction, has the unfortunate consequence of being taken too literally.

But evil, I suggest, has no real being of its own, certainly no personal ontology, for God created only that which was good. Lucifer, the morning star of God's creation, was not content to be a creature, but wished to be the Creator. This desire inverted the power of love that sustained him, and the love of power was born. Here Milton is powerfully convincing in his poetic insight that Lucifer wished to reign not to serve, to be a god not a creature. This craving for ultimate power, C. S. Lewis tells us, was the sin that the devil taught the human race.

So rebellion was born out of a good creature's free choice that turned on its Creator, disfiguring him and finally engorging him. Demonized by his own desire, the former angel of light is extinguished by his own darkness and the evil that emerges has no intrinsic life of its own, for it is parasitic on the forces and energies of God's good creation. Therefore the power of evil ultimately derives from the good power of God, but it is now corrupted power that has fallen away from His sustaining love. Having cast himself off from this love, that angelic being we call the devil loses not only his relationship with God, but is also out of sorts with himself—his own good nature. He drifts inexorably toward non-personhood, whose only end is nothingness—that existence of non-being which is outside the personal life of God.

As the devil has undergone his depersonalized metamorphosis—the carapace of evil hardening and usurping his good nature—he has become not more rational but irrational, not so much cunning as confused. He is diabolical but disordered, ferocious but fey, fearful but fickle, warlike but whimsical. In short, he has become all that God is not, and its instinct—for think more in terms of a mad beast than a personal agent—is to take as many of us with it as it can.

C. S. Lewis captures something of the eternal life of those who have fallen away from God in his book *The Great Divorce*,[32] where we find that outside the solidity and bright weight of heaven there is the Gray City where there is no substance or depth, only wraiths who cling to their illusions.

Can I furnish biblical verses to substantiate this exposition? I am sorry, but I cannot, for I hope it is obvious that I am just flying a kite: I am speculating on what the Bible chooses not to tell us. However, this is not an arbitrary exercise. I am trying to work through logically certain ideas on an understanding of God's personal revelation both in Jesus of Nazareth and as the triune God. His self-revelation as perfect love and personal communion also suggests its negotiations—being (or, more accurately, appearance of being) without communion, hate, and non-personhood. In other words, I am trying to do some serious theology, but only in the realm of legitimate guesswork.

Nevertheless, I am persuaded that the essence of spiritual warfare is not taking on demonic forces by binding strong men, destroying amulets and charms, and banning Halloween. Indeed, the passion with which some charismatics oppose All-Hallows Eve is matched only by their indifference to the celebration which follows it on All Saints' Day!

Perhaps it is only paranoia, but in my weaker moments I have a suspicion that the master Trickster has diverted us away from the battlefield to the games-room, where we indulge ourselves in spiritual fantasies and trivial pursuits while the real evil loosed on the world devours all that is good and decent with the heartlessness and cruelty of the Canaanite god Molech.

We may realize that we can fall prey to our own fantasies, and choose instead to step out from the closed world of our parishes and take to the streets and march for Jesus. Such a move could be a step in the right direction, for "coming out" is a way of "coming clean" with the public about charismatic intentions. But if we do decide to leave our sanctuaries and swarm on to the streets, we must strive to leave the paranoid universe behind, for otherwise we may imagine that by the very act of marching we are "shifting the demonic atmosphere" and "binding the strong men" of the city of Washington D.C. or the Mammon of materialistic America. And if we believe this, we may also come to believe that we can "bind"—and hence solve—unemployment, racism, or environmental decay by a stamp of our feet, a clenched fist in the air, or a shout to the skies.

We need to learn that there is more to exorcising the darkness than exercising our lungs. There is more to spiritual warfare than standing toe to toe with the devil and slugging it out. To meet like with like, or as Jesus puts it, evil with evil—or, if you prefer, power with more of the same—is to show that we have not really escaped the labyrinth of Dungeons and Dragons, He-Man, and the masters of the paranoid universe. If this were to be our approach to evil in the world, then it would be better if we stayed at home.

If my speculative theology of the parasitic nature of evil is correct, then perhaps attacking demons amounts to a welcoming party for them. Even some of our charismatic services can no longer begin until the demons are first "bound" in prayer. As an American charismatic recently put it: the devils take this as worship, and flock to hear themselves addressed. To put it bluntly, belligerence against them is not merely a welcoming, but a feast. (We can almost hear Screwtape telling Wormwood how he can wax fat on human aggression.) At the very least, to behave in this way is to descend to a sub-Christian barbarism. To exercise authority (*exousia* in the New Testament sense) over dark forces is one thing, but this is not the same as striving for greater fire-power to atomize the opposition (*dunamis*, a word rarely used in accounts of Christ's encounters with evil spirits, is over-played in charismatic vocabulary).

The violent comic-strip "blow the enemy away" youth culture of Judge Dread Law Enforcer seems to have found a responsive echo in the triumphalist charismatic camp. At a recent Charismatic Resources Exhibition, for example, there was a hot trade in T-shirts bearing the legend, "Jesus Christ Demon Crusher." I believe that genuine spiritual warfare means quite simply refusing to play the war game: we can only overcome evil with good, for if we appropriate the enemy's weapons we are lost. As Metropolitan Anthony puts it, "The devil does not care who you hate, even if it's himself." Power-seeking is dangerous, and the love of power is nothing less than devilish, for it corrupts Christian virtue.

Paradoxically, there is a more powerful way than power to dispel the gloom of demonic fear: lifting high the burning torch of God's love. How true the children's chorus is, "Jesus bids us shine with a clear, pure light, like a little candle burning in the night." God's love, the self-denying yet bright sacrificial love of Calvary, banishes the darkness as surely as the presence of Aslan melted the snows of Narnia. Jesus, by being nailed to a Roman cross, eschewed the way of violence and submitted to the powers—both human and spiritual. And yet, in His weakness, at His most vulnerable, He revealed God's way of true spiritual resistance to evil: and He rose victorious over sin, death, and the devil.

If we want to be victorious in spiritual warfare, it is not our place, nor is it possible for us, to die for the sins of the world—that battle has been fought and won once and for all by Christ. But the pattern of victory is the same for us, the followers of Jesus, as it was for our Lord. If we take up our cross, we too will discover that God's strength is made perfect in our weakness. We will also find that for us there is glory, but only by way of the cross.

The love of power is the way of the devil, and it is strong, triumphant, but transient. We can only defeat it with the power of love. Love is meek and lowly, but it is everlasting.

Four

The Faith Movement and the Question of Heresy

ANDREW WALKER, NIGEL WRIGHT, & TOM SMAIL

Our theological approach to the Charismatic movement in this book has been controversial yet conciliatory.[1] While we have looked for correctives, balance, and reflective criticism within the Renewal, this has not been conducted in a spirit of witch-hunting or inquisitorial menace. However, what sets the parameters for this type of theology to function properly, and what determines the rightness of our method, is the same as that which determined the nature of the theological task in the early Christian church. And that "what," that "something," we can best describe as "the dogmatic core"[2] of Christian faith.

At the heart of theology there is a nonnegotiable center of dogmatic truth, an unmovable residue of authoritative doctrine. We can properly call it the apostolic faith. The apostle Paul tells us that he came by it through the "revelation of Jesus Christ" (Galatians 1:12). Peter insists that "we did not follow cleverly invented stories when we told you about the power and coming of our Lord Jesus Christ, but we were eyewitnesses of his majesty" (2 Peter 1:16).

The essential truths of the received apostolic tradition were distilled by the early church into Christian charters or creeds (the Nicene Constantinopolitan Creed of AD 381 being the most ecumenical and authoritative). The apostolic faith in the creed contains what we might call "knowledge of revelation"—nonnegotiable truths gleaned from the Bible, or dogmas concerning the nature of God, the Trinity, the person and work of Christ, and the Church. It is only when theology contra-dicts the basic core truths of creedal Christianity that we can properly use the word heresy to describe it.[3]

When we turn to the modern charismatic movement and measure it against this creedal Christianity, we cannot really agree with the general tenor of John MacArthur's book *Charismatic Chaos*,[4] which considers charismatic Christianity to be more heretical than orthodox. On the contrary, we think it worth asserting that, on the whole, from the origins of classical Pentecostalism to the present-day Renewal there has been no significant deviation of the charismatic movement from what we earlier called "the dogmatic core" of Christian theology.[5] Perhaps the Christology of William Branham and indeed the whole "Latter Rain" theology of the late 1940s is problematic. But today the greatest concern must surely be reserved for the Word-of-Faith Move-ment.

The Faith Movement As Heresy

It is here that we need to move beyond our conciliatory approach to the sharp end of confrontational theology because of the central questions facing us in the Word-of-Faith Movement. Our question is not whether its proponents operate with unacceptable hermeneutics (which they do) nor even whether the whole thing is ethically dubious (which we believe it to be) but whether it is heresy: that is to say, does it deviate from the dogmatic core of apostolic faith? Regretfully we feel constrained to say that it probably does.

This is not the same as saying that brother X or pastor Y are self-conscious heretics. In the first place it is not so easy to determine who can properly be called the leaders of the Faith Movement. Benny Hinn, for example, has been associated with Faith teaching and many of his direct messages from the Holy Spirit, "revelation knowledge," echo Ken Hagin and Ken Copeland who are clearly self-confessed Faith teachers. Hinn, however, has publicly recanted some of his views and while we may be tempted to view it as disingenuous, he deserves, in charity, to be given the benefit of the doubt.

Indeed Hinn has done something all too rare among charismatic leaders: he has admitted that he has made mistakes and has agreed to change his views about some of the most controversial aspects of Faith teaching to which we shall shortly be turning:

"The Lord has been showing me some things I have been wrong about. At one time I taught certain things such as the "little gods" teaching, and Jesus dying spiritually. Now I have quit teaching such things, and I have made it clear that I no longer believe them."[6]

Hinn, however, provides a clue to the larger problem of identifying members of the Faith Movement (which is still colloquially called in many churches "health and wealth"). Like Hinn, many evangelists have stumbled across the Faith doctrines and have attempted to graft them on to their Pentecostal theology or incorporate them into their teaching programs. Once new teaching is out for all to see—especially teaching which claims spectacular results—it becomes part of the Pentecostal scene and is subject to the same copy-cat fashion that Andrew Walker will discuss later in Chapter 7 on miracles. We see similar teaching tendencies (though we are not suggesting they are identical) in the ministries of Morris Cerullo, Oral Roberts, and T. L. Osborn.[7] In Great Britain strong echoes of Faith teaching can be found in some of the so-called new churches and from evangelists as diverse as Colin Urquhart and Don Double.

It may well be that thousands of people who are promoting Faith doctrines, even sanitized ones, are innocents abroad. (Unwitting heretics, we should remind ourselves, are, strictly speaking, not heretics at all.) Unfortunately, if heretical doctrines are pressed into Christian service this means that if the source is tainted, then even innocents cannot avoid functioning as heretics.

Indeed we would go further. We have no idea whether acknowledged leaders of the Faith Movement, such as Kenneth Hagin, Kenneth Copeland, and Fred Price consciously deviate from orthodox Christianity (we are theologians not seers). We do not know if any of them have ever learned the ancient creeds or understand what constitutes the dogmatic core of Christianity.[8] We do know, however, that some of the central tenets of Faith teaching offends the dogmatic heart of historic orthodoxy. As a matter of fact, such teaching functions as heresy even if its teachers are not *de jure* heretics.

Tainted Sources and Gnostic Origins

Dan McConnell's book *A Different Gospel*[9] has built an overwhelming case that demonstrates how Ken Hagin plagiarized from the writings of E. W. Kenyon. McConnell further shows that the writings of Kenyon are clearly (though probably unconsciously) derived from the metaphysical cults of the late nineteenth century.[10] This might be unproblematic if such writings were secondary to Faith teaching, but they would appear to provide their very *raison d'etre*.

Writing in *Christianity Today*, one of us wrote some time ago that New Age thought has permeated liberal Christianity from the left in the form of the spiritual theology of Matthew Fox and has entered the right through the Faith Movement.[11] Such a statement is superficially true, but it fails to account for the diversity of ideas that informed those writings. Fox's work, for example, trawls from the neo-platonism of the Christian tradition as well as from contemporary paganism. The Faith Movement, on the other hand, is closer to the gnostic strains of Ralph Waldo Emerson and the Unity School of Christianity, the anti-materialism of Mary Baker Eddy, and the power of positive thinking of the cultic Science of the Mind. (The latter surfaces in different forms in the twentieth century from the "possibility theology" writings of Norman Vincent Peale and Robert Schuller to the "positive confession" statements of the Faith teachers.)

Although such phrases as New Thought Metaphysics have been used to describe such movements, they are not metaphysical and philosophical systems in the academic sense: they are movements that stress doctrines which are superior to the knowledge made possible through normal human faculties.

The nineteenth-century cults are by no means replications of early gnostic thinking but the echoes are unmistakable. When, for example, St. Irenaeus contested with the Gnostics of the second century they wanted to insist that salvation was only for the initiated few—those in possession of the gnosis (knowledge)—whereas Irenaeus insisted that salvation was for all, regardless of their intellectual status. Metaphysical cults, like Kenyon and the Faith Movement after them, stress spiritual knowledge as hidden from the conventional wisdom of religion and hence not available to the average person.

The Gnostics also believed that the material world was intrinsically evil and that human beings needed to escape from it into the superior spiritual realm through the mastery of esoteric techniques. They held the material world in such contempt that they sought to detach themselves from it either through extreme asceticism or through abuse of the body: some Gnostic sects, for example, encouraged rampant promiscuity on the grounds that sex was meaningless and without human dignity.

In the New Thought Metaphysics of the late nineteenth century, we find similar gnostic attitudes to the physical, created world: either it was acknowledged but shunned as in the secret doctrines of Madam Helene Blavatsky and Theosophy, or its reality was denied altogether as in the writings of Mary Baker Eddy and Christian Science. In both cases, however, the material world was something to be overcome not cherished.

The fact that the Faith Movement appears to be excessively materialistic through its emphasis on everlasting health and wealth should not deceive us, for appearances are often misleading. Faith teaching does not welcome God's good (though fallen) creation. When, for example, Kenneth Copeland talks of "victory," he stresses the overcoming of the physical and material limitations of life through "faith," which is nothing less than the supreme spiritual power, or force, of the universe. To exercise this faith it is necessary to act as the spiritual beings we essentially are.

Kenneth Hagin holds to a docetic or illusory view of human beings—reminiscent of Origen in the third century—seeing us (and indeed Jesus himself) as "spiritual man" wrapped in a body of flesh:

"Man is a spirit who possesses a soul and lives in a body. . . . Man at physical death leaves his body. Yet he is no less man than he was when he had his body."[12]

Of course we are not denying that part of the success of the Faith Movement is due to the fact that it feeds off the material longings of the American dream, but it also wins converts by promising to break the chains of necessity that bind us—turning us from wimps and ordinary little people (the tenor of contempt is never far away) into nothing less than "little gods."

The Faith Movement, like Kenyon before them, does not teach

humility (which in some patristic writings means "of the earth") or a celebration of our common humanity. In their understanding, the material world is not a good creation to be saved, but a fallen wasteland to be plundered. The cosmos is not yearning to be liberated, but it is coercible matter deserving to be bound by our power. Our bodies are not to be gloriously transfigured, but abandoned as empty and useless shells.

Concerning the Christian life itself it would seem for Kenyon that it is not Calvary Love that redeems but the great (hitherto hidden) truths of "revelation knowledge":

"When these truths really gain the ascendency in us, they will make us spiritual supermen, masters of demons and disease.... It will be the end of weakness and failure. There will be no more struggle for faith, for all things are ours. There will be no more praying for power, for He is in us ... In the presence of these tremendous realities, we arise and take our place. We go out and live as supermen indwelt by God."[13]

Hagin would suggest that we become ourselves not only as "little gods" but as much of an "incarnation" as Jesus of Nazareth![14]

Approaching Faith Movement Theology

Critics of Faith theology have a number of methodological problems to surmount before they begin to engage in polemical debate and start the perilous task of dogmatic assessment. First, a great deal of Faith teaching comes not through systematic presentation but in the form of audio and video tapes, television programs, and booklets.[15] Second, much of the Faith language, despite curious "spins" here and there, superficially appears to be consistant with Bible-belt theology. Third, a great deal of it is repetitive and rhetorical. Hagin quotes Kenyon (usually without citation) while Kenneth and Gloria Copeland re-package Hagin. Fred Price recycles it all with outrageous flourishes of his own:

"Now this is a shocker! But God has to be given permission to work in this earth realm on behalf of man.... Yes! You are in control! So, if man has control, who no longer has it? God.... God cannot do anything in this earth unless we let Him. And the way we let Him or give Him permission is through prayer."[16]

Fourth, as we saw at the beginning of this chapter, it is not altogether clear who is in the Faith Movement because so many evangelists and teachers have adapted aspects of it for themselves. Robert Tilton would seem to be an independent proponent of the prosperity gospel, but while evangelists Benny Hinn, Morris Cerullo, and Paul Crouch of Trinity Broadcasting obviously buy into Faith teaching it is by no means clear to us that they buy all of it.

Given these problems we have decided to concentrate on the teach-ings common to Hagin and Copeland who are without doubt indebted to Kenyon, and are accepted by most observers as the main teachers of the Faith Movement. We are acquainted with four critical sources, all written by Pentecostals, that have comprehensively raised questions about the orthodoxy of Faith teaching.[17] Hank Hanegraaff's book, *Chris-tianity in Crisis*, which is the most recent, is written for the man and woman in the pew and has risen to bestseller status. It is comprehen-sively documented and sensitive to dogmatic issues.

Our greatest debt is to Dan McConnell's book, *A Different Gospel*.[18] McConnell rightly shows that so-called revelation knowledge is a rad-ical dualism that positions spiritual truth as over and above the knowl-edge gained through normal human faculties. There also seems to be a tendency in Faith circles to talk of *rhema* knowledge as separate from *logos* knowledge. This can mean a direct knowledge of God that needs no scriptural mediation or legitimation. Even if, more positively, *rhema* is understood to be complementary to the *logos* of scripture, there is no significant exegetical case for separating *rhema* from *logos* in the New Testament.

McConnell highlights the unacceptable heightened spiritual dualism of Faith teaching. If we have been concerned in this book with the dualism of certain exorcists, and even John Wimber, who overplay the kingdom of darkness against the kingdom of light, this pales into insig-nificance at the role Satan plays in Faith teaching. This role may formally avoid metaphysical dualism but not functionally. In *Christianity in Crisis*, Hanegraaff tellingly uses the phrase "the deification of Satan" to high-light the devil's godlike status in Faith teaching.[19] God, in Faith teaching, appears not to be in control: He is duped by Satan in the Garden of Eden, has to resort to tricks to defeat Satan in hell, and is subject to the force of faith power that appears to be a principle of the universe greater than He.

The view that faith is a principle or force rather than a gracious unmerited gift of God is one of the most worrying features of Faith teaching. Manipulating this "faith force" smacks more of the occult than of Christian faithfulness. We are back in the realm of technique and gnosis. The fact, also, that faith for Hagin and Copeland has two poles, the positive confession, and the negative confession, is more than a little reminiscent of Christian Science.

It is a distinct possibility that positive confession of healing can be a delusion (if you are in fact ill). In addition, the so-called practice of negative confession (refusing to announce that you are healed when the word of healing has been spoken) can be used against you if you stay sick. This may produce a terrible guilt so great that physical suffering is augmented by psychological and spiritual pain. Negative confession is also, we must realize, an unassailable device to explain why in fact you are not healed. The whole issue is presented by Faith teachers almost as a syllogistic form of bogus Aristotelian logic:

Premise One: Those who confess that they are healed will be healed.

Premise Two: Those who do not confess their healing will stay sick.

Conclusion: Therefore all those who are not healed have made negative confession.

We could go on in this polemical vein *ad nauseum*, but in order to highlight the dogmatic issues at stake we would like to take the Faith doctrine of Atonement as a case study in doctrinal deviation from the apostolic faith. We follow and extrapolate from McConnell's masterful critique.

The Atonement in Word-of-Faith Theology

The doctrine of the Atonement has been hailed, from the time of Kenyon to present-day Faith teaching, as a mystery unfolded. It is not something, as Copeland puts it, that you will have picked up from your church tradition. This is indicative of gnostic theology. According to the Faith teachers there is a secret doctrine, forgotten or repressed, that these men have first had revealed to them by God and then confirmed for them by the fresh reading of old biblical texts and neglected Christian doctrines. Like Benny Hinn, both Hagin and Copeland are able to make great play of the fact that "revelation knowledge" (itself a phrase invented by Kenyon) comes to them initially through supernatural ex-periences—direct conversations with Jesus, angels, or the Spirit.[20]

Much of this "revealed knowledge" actually comes from Kenyon's book *What Happened From the Cross to the Throne*.[21] Hagin and Copeland paraphrase and explicate this in various ways. Most Christians, the story goes, have not realized that God is *not* Lord of the world: legally it belongs to Satan who tricked God out of its ownership in the Garden of Eden. Consequently God has no rights on earth, which is the devil's domain.

The gospel story continues in more or less traditional fashion (usu-ally less), but when we get to Golgotha very strange things begin to happen. At Calvary, Jesus of Nazareth dies on the cross but His physical sufferings and broken body do not in themselves atone for the sins of the world. (Fred Price once said that if it was suffering God wanted then the two thieves on either side of Jesus could have done the trick.)[22]

In 1 Peter 1:18–19 it states that we are redeemed "with the precious blood of Christ . . ." And yet Copeland is on record as saying that "when His blood poured out, it did not atone."[23]

The Bible also tells us that when Jesus died on the cross,

"Jesus called out with a loud voice, 'Father, into your hands I commit my spirit.' When he had said this, he breathed his last" (Luke 23:46).

Hagin, against all the scriptural evidence, insists that Jesus died twice. He died physically just like any human being would who was subjected to a crucifixion. But *before* that he died spiritually. (Price thinks it may even have been in the Garden of Gethsemane.) Jesus had to die spiritually, so the doctrine goes, because the source of sickness, sin, and indeed poverty, is spiritual and not physical.

This spiritual death (the first death) cut Jesus off from God. The spiritually dead Jesus then became not only sin for us, but in being made sin He also took upon himself the nature of Satan (which Faith teachers insist all fallen human beings share through the Fall) and suffered the curse of the law—which is no less than sin, sickness, and poverty. God's identification with fallen human beings under the curse of the law Kenyon and Hagin see as the legal identification of Christ with us.

It is an at-one-ment with the consequences of the high treason of Adam in the Garden of Eden and the subsequent satanic (fallen) nature of humankind. In becoming satanic, like us, Christ has fulfilled God's legal obligation to respect the devil's dominion over the world. In short, Satan has rights, and God both recognizes and respects them. The doctrine is more emphatic in Copeland's version of it for, according to him, Satan actually overpowered Jesus on the cross so that God is, temporarily at least, defeated and consequently a failure.[24]

After His two-stage death Jesus descends into hell a broken, defeated victim of torture. Hanegraaff is so offended by Copeland's description of our Lord as He enters hell that he cannot resist quoting it as often as he can. "His [Jesus] emaciated, poured out, little, wormy spirit is down in the bottom of that thing [hell]."[25]

But Satan overreached himself, for only sinners can be dragged into hell. Jesus was innocent of wrongdoing so God was able to take advantage of Satan's complicity and defeat him through his own duplicity. Just as Satan tricked God in the Garden, God tricks Satan in the bowels of hell. The devil having exceeded his rightful jurisdiction entitles God, legally, to act and speak His word of faith into hell.

Jesus, dead in sin and wrapped in Satan's nature, was now able to be "born again" in hell, or reborn spiritually. God turns the tables on Satan, and Jesus is reconnected to His disconnected spirit:

"He [Jesus] was literally being reborn before the devil's very eyes. He began to flex His spiritual muscles.... Jesus was born again—the firstborn from the dead the Word calls Him—and He whipped the devil in his own backyard ...."[26]

It follows, as a consequence of Christ's spiritual rebirth, that we too can be reborn spiritually and become an incarnation of Jesus, a little god. This is Kenyon's reverse side of the law of identification. God has legally fulfilled His role—now we, through faith, can fulfil ours. Kenyon calls this "vital" as opposed to legal identification. It is, if you will, our part in our at-one-ment with Christ: we can appropriate, through faith, God's victory for ourselves. Vital identification, however, turns out to be more than claiming the promises of faith: it is no less than a full-blown form of deification—taking upon ourselves the divine nature of God.

It follows also that once we have become reborn, spiritually incarnated as little Christs, we can have access, in our true spiritual natures, to faith force—the true force of the universe—and "whip the devil" with superior power, for God (that also now means us) is in control of the world (again).

Hagin tells us that he asked God for many things over forty-five years of ministry, and God always answered and the answer was always yes. For men and women reborn in the Spirit nothing is impossible, for they are free from Satan's nature, and equipped with Faith principles— the very stuff that rules the universe.

Christians, says Hagin, can write their own ticket with God if they follow the four principles of positive confession that he received directly from Jesus in a vision. (To us, these look like gnostic formulas.) The principles are (1) Say it (2) Do it (3) Receive it (4) Tell it.[27] We might think that four principles, like four laws, or three steps to heaven, have little relevance in the Christian life unless they can be directly linked to personal knowledge of God. Apparently, however, according to Hagin at least, even sinners can follow the four principles of successful living, for they are written into the very laws of the universe.

What are we to make of all of this? In order to decide we need to sift the dogmatic issues from the polemical and hermenuetical ones, but as we shall show, the misreading of Christian tradition enables the Faith teachers falsely to legitimize their controversial theology.

The dogmatic issues are these: (1) However we understand the Atonement, the dogmatic position of historic Christianity is that Jesus atones for the sins of the world in and through His incarnation, culminating in the Easter Passion. In short, Jesus atones in the flesh as an event in space and time, not out of this world in a spirit (timeless) realm. Doctrines not grounded in history but set adrift into timeless spirituality and paganism are not Judaism or Christianity.

(2) To say that Jesus died twice is an absurdity, and to say that He died spiritually is, at best, misleading, and, at worst, it is heresy. According to the Council of Chalcedon, Jesus has two natures in one person. As a human being, as the man from Nazareth, Jesus dies—the two natures are temporarily rended. But as the Logos, the uncreated second person of the Trinity, Jesus is consubstantial with the Father (Nicene Creed) and He lives eternally with Him before, during, and after His incarnation in the material world of creation. To say that Jesus died spiritually is also to say that the Faith Movement does not have a

high Christology for, to repeat ourselves, at no time does Jesus cease to be the Logos.[28]

(3) Such an unorthodox and low Christology inevitably leads to an incoherent doctrine of the Holy Trinity. Did the Trinity become temporarily a binary unity when Jesus died? Faith teaching does not formally teach such a doctrine to our knowledge, but it is a logical consequence of their doctrine of the spiritual death of Jesus.

We wonder also, Who or What is the Holy Spirit in Faith teaching? Is He the "Lord and giver of life" as the Nicene Creed puts it, the third person of the blessed Trinity, or is He reduced to God's power force [29] or reduced yet again to that universal principle, faith force?

(4) It is entirely without biblical foundation to say that when Jesus was made "to be sin for us" (2 Corinthians 5:21), He became ensnared in Satan's nature. The Jesus who dies on the cross cannot be characterized as a demoniac for He is the God-Man, holy, without sin, "a lamb without blemish or defect" (1 Peter 1:19). In being "made" sin for us Jesus neither willingly sinned nor in bearing our sins on the tree did He become corrupted by sin.

The fact that Jesus "took the rap" for our sins does not mean that in the merciful act of taking them He was transformed into sin itself. St. Irenaeus in a more traditonal image understands our Lord uniting himself to sinful humanity without being contaminated by it. To illustrate his point he uses the story of Jesus touching and healing the leper without becoming himself leprous.

(5) There is no scriptural warrant or canonical foundation for saying that Jesus is reborn in hell. It is not only metaphysical fiction, it falsely proclaims that Jesus atones for sin outside of His incarnational life. Atonement, for the Faith teachers, is not achieved on the cross (where Jesus was defeated by Satan) but in hell. This victory was won not through the intrinsic goodness of Jesus, or by the unique graciousness of the God-Man. On the contrary, it is achieved because of God's legal identification with us on the cross, which catches Satan off guard and allows God to pull a fast one over His arch rival in hell. With such a theology we are in the realm of trickster tales like some Brer Rabbit getting one over on Brer Bear.

(6) Historical Christianity does not teach that Jesus was reborn, or reincarnated in hell. Thus we cannot believe that His followers can be

reborn in the spirit plane (as if they could enter some other dimension outside earthly existence) and become reincarnations of Christ, or little gods in their own right. Such a view, as we shall argue, is not what 2 Peter 1:4 means when the apostle used the daring phrase "that ... you may participate in the divine nature."

Lessons From Church History

Dogmatic theology necessitates a knowledge of the Christian tradition. Church historians will notice that Faith teaching is far from being a new revelation, or a rediscovery of lost traditions; it is in fact a conflation, and misreading, of three early church doctrines: (1) The Greek Fathers' speculation that the ransom paid for our sins by Jesus was a debt to the devil. (This does indeed have a "trickster" flavor to it.) (2) The descent into hell by Jesus after the crucifixion. (3) The doctrine of *theosis*—deification, or perhaps less misleadingly, the divinization of Christian believers who "have clothed yourselves with Christ" (Galatians 3:27).

The Faith teachers, via Kenyon, have not been faithful to the early church traditions of the ransom theory, the descent into hell, or divinization. Indeed they may not even be completely aware of them (though they clearly have inklings of such teachings).[30]

What in fact they have done is take three strands of early Christian theology (picked up originally by Kenyon from somewhere), twisted them, weaved them together with metaphysical cultic twine and hermeneutical guile, and created a syncretistic tapestry of heretical nonsense.

Let us briefly look at these three strands of early church doctrine. The first thing to say is that all three doctrines are not necessarily crucial to the doctrinal core of apostolic tradition but are rather expressions of theological opinion (*theologuemena*). If the Faith teachers simply taught these doctrines as part of a rounded Christian theology, then, although we might wish respectfully to disagree with them, we would have no right to accuse them of heresy.

(1) The Ransom Theory

Neither the Nicene, Apostles', or Athanasian Creed of the early centuries theorizes in any way about the Atonement: The fact of it was taken as a reference point for apostolic faith, but as no major disputes arose concerning the work of Christ in the early Christian centuries the creeds have little to say about it.[31] The so-called classical theory of atonement,[32] which was never worked out in any systematic way, emphasized the overcoming of the devil by Christ on the cross and, as has been said in Chapter 3, there is adequate scriptural warrant for this approach.

However, some of the Greek Fathers (and Western authorities too) believed that when 1 Timothy 2:6 says that Christ gave himself "a ransom for all" the ransom was paid to the devil (certainly not a vengeful God). This belief was strongly supported by St. Gregory of Nyssa who maintained that the devil held rights (in the sense of legal title) over the world, and God being a just God, had to pay the devil his dues in order to win back His lost territory. For Nyssa, and later St. Augustine, God tricks the devil out of his inheritance rather like Jacob tricks Esau out of his. Or looking at it with less duplicity: God knew the law better than the devil, just as Aslan knew, better than the White Witch, that there was an even deeper magic in Narnia which could defeat her own strong magic. (See C. S. Lewis' *The Lion, the Witch, and the Wardrobe*.[33])

There are three things to say about this. First, Nyssa's friend, St. Gregory of Nazianzus, rejected this train of thought. For him, the devil was a robber and a thief and could not be said to have any rights over the world. Nazianzus is the second great theologian of the Eastern church (the first being St. John of the Gospel), and as such clearly represents the more acceptable view in the Orthodox churches even to this day.

Second, in time, in both East and West, the ransom theory fell into disuse (if not disrepute) not only because of its weak exegetical basis but because it failed adequately to deal with the full complexity and grandeur of the Atonement. Henceforth in the West the juridical theory of the Atonement predominates (especially after the tenth century), while in the East Irenaeus's incarnational atonement holds sway (in which there is not only a *reconciliatio* in Christ but a *recapitulatio*).

Third, and this is the point of dogmatic significance, the ransom paid to the devil in early church theories takes place unequivocally on the cross and not in hell. St. Gregory of Nyssa in his Great Catechetical Oration talks of Jesus as being the bait on the hook (the cross), while

Augustine follows Nyssa's idea but employs a different metaphor:

"The devil jumped for joy when Christ died; and by the very death of Christ the devil was overcome: he took, as it were, the bait in the mousetrap. . . . The Lord's cross was the devil's mousetrap; the bait which caught him was the death of the Lord."[34]

(2) The Descent Into Hell

Actually the phrase "descended into hell" is not to be found in the Bible or the Nicene Creed though it does appear in both the Athanasian and the Apostles' Creed (which the Faith teachers know full well). The patristic understanding of Jesus' "descent," however, had nothing to do with His spiritual death, His humiliation, His rebirth, or His suffering. They were trying to make sense of Peter's words when he says that the Spirit who had brought Jesus back from the dead also enabled Him to "preach to the spirits in prison" (1 Peter 3:19).

The Greek Fathers, Cyril of Jerusalem in particular, clearly saw the hell to which Christ descended as the place of the dead, and they had adequate biblical warrant on their side, for besides 1 Peter 3:19 there is also 1 Peter 4:6 to back it up:

"For this is the reason the gospel was preached even to those who are now dead, so that they might be judged according to men in regard to the body, but live according to God in regard to the spirit."[35]

The Fathers believed that the triumphant God in Christ harrows hell, enlightening it with the power of the Spirit of God and rescuing the dead who had fallen asleep under the old covenant of Grace. In this sense, to recapitulate and extend our earlier remarks, hell is to be understood as a limbo, or death's domain, rather than the eternal fire of damnation. As the Paschal Troparian puts it:

"Christ is risen from the dead, trampling down death by death, and upon those in the tombs bestowing life."

Calvin, in his *Institutes of the Christian Religion*, grants that great authorities have taught the harrowing of hell but he considers it only a story. Nevertheless, Calvin wished to uphold the orthodoxy of the descent into hell because he believed that Christ had to suffer God's condemnation even in death. The great Reformer wanted to say that Christ suffered the "agony of death" (Acts 2:24), for he believed that this phrase indicated that Jesus suffered the full wrath of God in hell.[36]

It may very well be that Calvin's view of hell was influenced by

Dante and the medieval translation of the Greek *Hades* or the Hebrew *Sheol* into the altogether more horrific Latin *Inferno*. Of greater certainy is the fact that the notion of the Father punishing the Son in hell owes much to Anselm's juridical theory of the Atonement in the tenth century.

The theological issue is this: whether we choose to follow Cyril of Jerusalem or Calvin in their interpretation of the biblical texts on "descent," neither reading supports Word-of-Faith teaching that Jesus accomplishes victory in hell as opposed to the cross.

(3) The Doctrine of *Theosis*

Although the language is strange to most of us there is a biblical basis, the Eastern Orthodox church would argue, for the deification of Christian believers. What else does Peter mean, they would say, when he tells us in 2 Peter 1:4 that through the great and precious promises "you may be partakers of the divine nature, having escaped the corruption that is in the world through lust"? Many of the Greek Fathers took it to mean that just as God became one of us, we may, through adoption by the Spirit into Christ, become not merely like Him but joined to Him. The use of the Pauline phrase the "body of Christ" suggests to us an organic connection to Jesus the head of the Church.

However, in typical Greek rhetorical style, from Athanasius in the fourth century to Maximus in the eighth, the Fathers would say that "God became man in order that man may become God." Understandably neither the Catholic nor Protestant West have been too happy with this language: it seems to suggest total identification between God and His creation. Or to a modern evangelical mind it smacks of Hinduism or extreme panentheism.

Two remarks are in order that are pertinent to our thesis. First, the Fathers never meant to say that being adopted by the Spirit into the body of Christ, the Church, meant that Christians were, or ever could be, identical to Christ—though we are identified with Him as the firstborn (the new Adam) of a glorious redeemed humanity. To be members of Christ's body is not the same as being absorbed into the Holy Trinity in such a way that we become all that God is. The transcendent God invites us to the eternal dance of the divine Trinity, if you will, but as created, though adopted, partners (part-takers), never as uncreated equals. God remains in His gracious dealings with us what

He always has been—a transcendent other.

Second, the patristic position never suggests for a moment that we are equal to God in either power or spiritual prowess. Even the idea of saints in the Catholic tradition is meant to suggest that there are those further along the path than the rest of us (perfected, in Wesleyan terms), not people who possess a different spiritual nature to ordinary men and women.

Crucially, the possibility of partaking in the divine nature was understood by the Fathers to be eschatological not economical: i.e., it is in heaven that we obtain our full glory, not in created existence. At the last judgment we will be able to see Christ as He is because we will have been physically raised to our true spiritual stature as redeemed men and women.

In contrast we see that Word-of-Faith *theosis* (a technical term they never use to our knowledge) is something to be experienced now. We are, to recall Hagin's words, essentially "spirit" beings and it is in "the spirit" that the faith force is released where we become the "little gods." (Given this spiritual realm, where we can be released from the restrictions, necessities, and confinements of material time, we wonder if a doctrine of the physical resurrection is really necessary?)

What we are asserting is that the doctrine of deification taught by the Faith Movement is not the teaching of the Greek Fathers (which is either rejected or misunderstood by most Western Christians anyway) but is akin to what the metaphysical cults teach. We do not mean to say that Faith teaching is spiritualistic in any overt sense, but that it is nevertheless a spiritual or gnostic doctrine rather than an incarnational and Christian one.

Faith theology appears to be materialistic, then, but is in fact spiritualistic, whereas, in ironic contrast, patristic theology and its Eastern Orthodox embodiment today appears to be a mystical religion to an Occidental eye but is (above all) an incarnational one which preaches that salvation is of the flesh. "Therefore since Christ suffered in his body..." (1 Peter 4:1). To use modern terminology, Orthodoxy shares with all Western Christians who hold to the dogmatic core of apostolic faith, a belief in the Atonement as salvation history, not spiritual mystery.

Since New Testament times pagan movements have arisen that seem to shadow Christianity and sometimes interpenetrate it. From the Gnostic sects, through to the Neoplatonism of the early Middle Ages, we come across teachings that are immanentist rather than transcendent, elitist rather than all-embracing, spiritualist rather than materialist. The New Thought Metaphysics of the late nineteenth and early twentieth century gave new life and form to these shadowy religions and taught the existence of an alternative universe of absolute reality where spiritual power lies outside material creation and created time.

Unwittingly, we believe, Faith teaching feeds off these higher spiritual doctrines. Although they seek to justify their orthodoxy through biblical proof texts and appeals to a hidden Christian tradition, we hope that we have shown via our brief case study that, in the instance of the Atonement, what emerges is a muddle of Christian tradition clouded by heretical conclusions concerning the person, nature, and work of Christ.

Conclusion

If Faith teaching was merely silly we would need to do nothing but keep silent or gently expose its idiosyncracies. When Copeland tells us, for example, that God is ... "very much like you and me. A being that stands somewhere around 6'2", 6'3", that weighs somewhere in the neighborhood of a couple of hundred pounds, little better, [and] has a [hand] span of nine inches across,"[37] our natural reaction is to gawk in disbelief, not to hurl anathemas.

But heresy is about spiritual corruption, not merely muddled thinking. How many people have died who made a positive confession but refused to take medical advice? How many earnest souls thought they were joining the spiritual elite and ended up spiritually desolate? Will we ever know how many people gambled on the lottery of positive financial confession and ended up bankrupt? Who can count the numbers of all those who have put their faith in Faith and lost what little faith they had?

Recently Pastor Jack Hayford has urged a more gracious approach to the Faith Movement. Even though he believes it is essential to maintain biblical orthodoxy, he wishes to work for reconciliation rather than confrontation, for healing rather than savaging, for charity rather than hate.[38] He is right in all these things.

However, problems remain which no amount of conciliatory theology or charity can resolve. Pastor Desmond Cartwright, the official historian of the Elim Pentecostal church, once told us at a C. S. Lewis Centre workshop that Pentecostalism suffers from the besetting sin of pragmatism: if something is successful, he argued, many Pentecostals/charismatics will think it is probably of God and they will support it. Pastor Cartwright's conviction is that we often allow our natural desire for success to swamp our spiritual and theological good sense.

We would add two things to these wise remarks. First it is a great mistake to assume that if you are a charismatic then you will be closer to charismatics than other Christians. If one speaks in tongues, some feel, this is the equivalent to having gained entrance to a "believers club" that somehow ensures orthodoxy. But tongue-speaking may be demonic, or psychologically induced,[39] and even when it is not, glossolalia does not exempt us from acquiring sound theology which is rooted in the Bible and the communal experience of the church militant.

Furthermore, do Methodists assume that they are one with their fellow Methodists in a denomination where extreme liberalism and fundamentalism coexist with many shades in between? Are Episcopalians of one mind because they are in the same church? The question the charismatic movement needs to ask itself about the Faith Movement is not is it Pentecostalist in some way, but is it authentic charismatic Christianity that is loyal to the dogmatic core of historical orthodoxy?

Secondly, we know only too well that to criticize co-religionists is seen as judgmental and against the Spirit of Christ. But there is a great deal of hypocrisy here and a great deal of fear.

There is fear because sometimes when we claim not to be offending charity we are in fact afraid of retaliation from popular religious leaders. "Touch not mine anointed" is a much abused biblical injunction (1 Chronicles 16:22) and can be the voice not only of the Lord but of the scoundrel. It can also be the language of power, of subjugation, or the last resort of the demagogue. How can we, for example, take the following words of Kenneth Copeland as anything other than a threat:

"There are people attempting to sit in judgment right today over the ministry that I'm responsible for, and the ministry that Kenneth E.

Hagin is responsible for.... Several people that I know had criticized and called that faith bunch out of Tulsa a cult. And some of 'em are dead right today in an early grave because of it, and there's more than one of them got cancer."[40]

There is hypocrisy because some charismatic Christians do not hesitate to condemn those on the liberal left but they will not stand up against heresy on the right. If we speak out against the sects outside our ranks, should we not condemn the cults in our midst? This is not offending against charity for we are not castigating individuals from a position of moral superiority: we are, which is the task of dogmatic theology, "standing on the promises of God."

As modern theologians, we do not possess the authority of an apostle Paul who did not hesitate to hurl curses at those who preached a different gospel (Galatians 1:6–9). As teachers, however, we can and must stand with the great apostle Peter and warn, in sobriety, and without fear or malice, of dangerous teaching "which ignorant and unstable people distort, as they do the other Scriptures" (2 Peter 3:16).

TWO

Issues for Renewal— Practical Considerations

FIVE

In Spirit and in Truth:
Reflections on Charismatic Worship

TOM SMAIL

Because charismatic renewal is about our relationship to God, the renewal of our worship of God is one of its primary concerns, and in fact over the last twenty-five years it has had a transforming effect on the worship of all the churches. Very many congregations, irrespective of their denominational allegiance or liturgical tradition and whether or not they would be content to describe themselves as charismatic, have begun to sing the songs that the renewal has taught them and have entered into at least some of the immediacy, intimacy, freedom, and joy in the near presence of God that, through the renewal, the Holy Spirit has been restoring to us.

At the center of that worship has been a new release of praise with its own distinctive characteristics that have supplemented and complemented the cherished treasury of worship that the churches have inherited from the past. In this connection, it is no accident that the distinctive feature of charismatic worship, which has made a positive impression on most people who have come into contact with it, has been the corporate and spontaneous singing in tongues that has often been called "singing in the Spirit." This seems to me to be the quintessence of worship in its charismatic mode, because, although it may happen quite infrequently and may only last for a very few minutes, when it does, it gives expression to the distinctive features of renewal worship that characterizes it as charismatic.

Singing in the Spirit bypasses the rational faculties; it reminds us that alongside the praise of the renewed mind there is the praise of the renewed heart that, when it is being evoked by the Spirit, expresses not simply our superficial feelings, but engages the deep primal emotions at the hidden center of our being in our self-offering to the living God. Such praise is direct, spontaneous, and simple. It escapes from a complicated conceptuality and a secondhand dependence on such liturgical resources as prayerbooks and hymnbooks, and responds in immediacy and freedom to the contact with the living Lord that the Spirit makes possible and, in joyous serenity, rejoices in and mediates upon His poured-out grace and His revealed glory.

If singing in the Spirit exemplifies these features in their purest form, nevertheless, when the renewal widens its worship to embrace again the spoken word and the formulated confession of praise in hymn or chorus, much of the immediacy, simplicity, and deep meditational quality are still in evidence. Jeremy Begbie reminds us that the renewal has not only added to our stock of songs of its own, which he describes as "songs of intimacy" and "songs of hushed reverence," which speak of God's nearness and of an intense encounter between God and the worshiper, these have words that convey a sense of awe at being in God's presence, and are sung to music that is generally tender and very slow. Such songs, he adds, "have very few parallels in traditional hymnody." Begbie's article, "The Spirituality of Renewal Music"[1] is a brief but authoritative study of its subject which, in its descriptions and assessments, breaks new ground in this whole matter.

Those of us who have actually participated in charismatic renewal worship, especially in its early days and our own early days in it, can bear witness that we have been carried, not into some vague mystic ecstasies without Christian content, but into the kind of worship of the Ancient of Days and of the Lamb who is in the midst of His throne that the book of Revelation describes. This has added to our corporate worship of God a dimension of immediacy, directness, depth, freedom, and joy to an extent that we did not know before.

From our experiences of such worship we are left in little doubt that it is the Holy Spirit who in these special times and ways has drawn us so deeply and engrossingly into the praiseful worship of the Father and the Son. According to the New Testament, God has sent the Spirit of His Son into our hearts precisely that He may cry, "Abba, Father" and teach us to cry it for ourselves after Him (Galatians 4:6; Romans 8:15). It is by the same Spirit and in the same accents of praise that we confess that Jesus Christ is Lord, to the glory of God the Father (cf. Philippians 2:11; 1 Corinthians 12:3). In the kind of praise of Abba Father and the Lord Jesus into which the renewal has led us, we recognize the same Spirit who was at work in the New Testament churches at work in us.

Nevertheless, while we have every reason to speak with great gratitude of charismatic worship, we have at the same time to recognize that at the moment all is not well with it. Often in the seminars out of which this book emerged we heard ministers and leaders who had been deeply involved in the renewal and its worship over long periods express perplexity and dismay that somehow or other the glory had departed from it; that the high praise of God had degenerated into endless repetitive chorus-singing that was in danger of becoming a bore and a burden rather than a release and a joy; that the celebration of the saving acts of God had been replaced by pious self-indulgence in relig-ious sentiment for its own sake; that people were sometimes being worked up and manipulated into a strained and artificial worship that concealed God's absence more than it responded to His presence; that the thirst for miraculous healings and dramatic prophecies could dull people's appetite for God's Word; that in the midst of the noisy and exuberant striving for the spiritual mountaintops there was little room for silent listening and patient waiting upon God.

Furthermore, if we stand back a little and measure modern charis-matic spirituality against the whole tradition of Christian worship in all its varied liturgical expressions, we shall see that the charismatics, as well as having valuable contributions and indeed corrections to make, have lacks and defects to be remedied and filled. And, remembering our previous discussion, we shall perhaps not be too surprised to discover that these are the very defects that can easily spring from a *theologia gloriae* that does not wrestle with a *theologia crucis*, and can engender a worship style that concentrates too one-sidedly on the triumphs of Easter and Pentecost and does not sufficiently take into account that they can be reached only by way of the cross.

Bearing that in mind, charismatics need to ask themselves whether it is possible that their very joy in their direct and immediate relationship to God in the Spirit might make them forget that God's saving act that makes that relationship possible was done without our having any part of it or feelings about it, indirectly and in our absence long ago, when Jesus gave himself for us on the cross. We need to incorporate into our worship the realization that the event on which our salvation wholly depends was not done *in* us by the Spirit, but *for* us by Jesus at Calvary, and that everything else follows from and depends on that. Worship must have a place not just for the moments when hearts lift high and eyes are shining and joy abounds, but for the dull days when we are empty and unresponsive in ourselves and can only hold out empty hands for the bread and wine, the body and blood, the redeeming gift of His living but crucified self that Jesus gives us from the cross.

When I taught at St. John's College, Nottingham, I worshiped most days in the charismatic exuberance of the college chapel, but I was glad every Sunday to be part of a local parish of distinctly catholic churchmanship, where I was not under any pressure to shine with joy or glow with gifts, but was constantly reminded in the sacrament that, however I might be feeling or faring, what Christ had done on Calvary was done forever and was available for me.

Second, and closely connected with this, is the failure of charismatics to find a central and regular place in their worship for the confession of sins and deep repentance that God's free forgiveness evokes from us and creates in us. The charismatic renewal was in part a healthy reaction against a sin-centered piety that, in its distinctive evangelical and catholic forms, was so imbued with a sense of God's holiness and our unworthiness that it failed to emphasize that God in Christ was so undeservedly and munificently gracious to the unworthy that He not only freely forgave them but blessed them with His Spirit, His gifts, His fruits, and His power. That was a needed correction, but itself stands in need of radical correction if an absorbing preoccupation with our experiences of the Spirit ever lets us forget that we are sinners who, every time we approach God, need not only to praise Him for His gifts but to confess our sins and to repent of them. That is how we can be constantly renewed in our whole relationship to Him, so that what

He gives us in the Spirit is not soiled, distorted, and misused in our sin-stained hands.

It is often remarked that every great renewal in the Spirit begins when He convicts Christ's people of their sins and leads them to repentance (cf. John 16:8–11). This has not so far been characteristic of the charismatic renewal, and the lack of it explains the impression of superficiality and even unreality that the renewal and its worship can sometimes convey. It is highly unsatisfactory, and indeed can be dangerous and disruptive, as 1 Corinthians makes clear, when gifts are prized but sins remain unconfessed and unrepented of and, as a consequence, lives remain unchanged.

Third, in charismatic worship, intercession is subordinated to praise. We have to be careful to define exactly what we are saying at this point. Because the Holy Spirit is at work in the charismatic renewal, and because He is himself an interceding Spirit, who "intercedes for the saints in accordance with God's will" (Romans 8:27), there is no doubt that He has led many charismatics into a new and deep ministry of intercession. Furthermore, if we look at the Lord's Prayer, we shall see that there is a sense in which intercession for human needs is secondary to the affirmation and praise of God. We hallow His name, His kingdom, and His will before we pray for provision, pardon, and protection for ourselves. Many of us have discovered that meaningful intercession can be undertaken only after we have reminded ourselves, through affirming praise, of the nature and character of the God to whom we are praying, thus settling our asking within the context of His name, His kingdom, and His will.

But, with all that said, it remains true that corporate charismatic worship, which is our main present concern, has often neglected the hard work of intercession. If it is true that praise must precede petition, it is equally true that petition has to spring from praise, and that does not always happen. Charismatics tend to concentrate on the exercise of a ministry of healing rather than engaging in prayer for healing. In such a ministry of healing, we tend to see ourselves as standing, as it were, at God's side and exercising the power and authority that He has given us against illness and evil, armed with words of knowledge and spiritual resources that will make us the triumphant masters of the situations we encounter.

We may contrast with that the kind of prayer for healing that takes a much more lowly stance, identifying less with the God who can meet the need than with the person whose need it is. Intercessors have faith in God, else they would not approach Him at all, or would approach Him without expectation, but they are deeply aware of their identification with those on whose behalf they pray, and with their perplexity and uncertainty as to what God is doing or is willing to do in that situation. In intercession we make other people's needs our own, and stretch out weak and empty hands that possess no power and ability to the God who has what we do not have and, on the word of Jesus, is willing to give it to us.

In other words, genuine intercession always has about it some of the agony of Gethsemane and the costly identification of Calvary, where, with Christ, we are helpless with the helpless and needy with the needy, and on their behalf we offer ourselves, our time, our energy, our concern, our love, acknowledging our total dependence on God and our humble waiting for Him to respond to us in ways and at times of His own choosing. It is when intercession has that Calvary dimension at the heart of it that the resurrecting answers can be given and the Easter triumphs can begin. To rush past the perplexing and demanding work of intercession, in which often, with Paul, "we do not know what we ought to pray for" (Romans 8:26), to the exercise of power gifts, can be a subtle way of evading the cross. It can also impede our awareness of and our response to the interceding ministry of the Spirit within us, for the passage just quoted reminds us that it is precisely when we enter into the humbling perplexities of intercession that "the Spirit helps us in our weakness" and "intercedes for us with groans that words cannot express." Charismatic worship needs to have room for the Spirit as humble intercessor, as well as for the Spirit of triumphant power.

We have been arguing that charismatic worship, as we have known it in the renewal, can often highlight our subjective response to God and neglect the objective work of salvation that Christ undertook on our behalf, and that it can marginalize the confession of sins and intercessory prayer. It would, however, be a thoroughly negative enterprise if we stopped short at drawing attention to such defects and one-sided overemphasis, unless we were to go on to make positive suggestions about how they might be corrected. It is encouraging to record that

these suggestions are being made from within the charismatic constituency itself, where people are increasingly realizing that the treasures
of renewal worship can best be conserved and enhanced, and its deficiencies overcome, by a rediscovery of its positive and creative relationship to the liturgical traditions of the church, insofar as they themselves faithfully reflect the biblical gospel in its teaching about and
implications for the worship of the God and Father of our Lord Jesus
Christ.

That freedom and liturgy are complementary to each other rather
than mutually exclusive alternatives can be attested both by experience
and by Scripture. Liturgy that has no room for the freedom and freshness
of a spontaneous spiritual response to God quickly hardens into ritualistic performance that becomes boring and irrelevant to everyone
except the conservative minorities who have invested their security in
it. On the other hand, worship that despises and rejects all liturgical
constraints either degenerates into licentious self-indulgence or, more
likely, without realizing what is happening, evolves liturgical forms of
its own that can become as strict and as constraining as any it has
rejected. Those of us who have attended many charismatic meetings in
many different contexts know that they are not always as spontaneous
and unscripted as they may appear. Certain songs sung in a certain
sequence can be guaranteed to produce singing in tongues that will be
followed by one of five predictable "prophecies" that we have all heard
before. To say that is not to be cynical, but simply to recognize that
liturgical shape is more integral to worship than we sometimes imagine,
and might at its best be itself a work and gift of the Spirit of God.

The positive connection between spiritual spontaneity and liturgical
structure is, I believe, implicit, in what Jesus is recorded as saying about
worship in the course of His conversation with the woman of Samaria
in John 4:24: "God is spirit, and his worshipers must worship in spirit
and in truth." To worship in spirit means to engage in worship that is
full of the immediacy, spontaneity, inward reality, and personal reality
that the Holy Spirit inspires. In other words, it is, in that sense, charismatic worship.

But we are also to worship "in truth," and, in this gospel, truth is
not thought of abstractly or philosophically, but concretely and practi-
cally. That which is true is that which is faithful to what God has

revealed and given in His only-begotten Son, who is himself personally the truth (John 14:6). Therefore, true worship is worship that is centered upon the truth as it has been personally and savingly revealed and enacted in Christ. It proclaims and receives the truth of Christ incarnate, crucified and risen, in scriptural word and gospel sacraments. In its praying and singing it responds appropriately to that truth and allows it to lead us into the praise, confession, intercession, and self-offering that it creates, evokes, and requires. In its liturgy the Church recognizes the givenness of the truth of the gospel and constructs the framework and the structures within which our response to the gospel can be freely and fully expressed. We worship God acceptably, not in any way that pleases us or is congenial to us, noting the fashions or impulses that the moment suggests, but when we allow God's mighty saving act in Christ to shape and reshape our response to it.

There is no doubt a certain tension in worship between spiritual spontaneity and liturgical givenness, between freedom and framework, and sometimes, as the charismatic renewal itself testifies, it will be necessary to focus on one factor rather than the other. If we are prisoners of the framework, we shall have to rediscover our freedom in the Spirit; if that freedom is in danger of leading us away from Christ into religious self-indulgence or one-sidedness, we shall have to return to the discipline and sobriety that the framework can offer.

This tension is, however, in the end creative and not destructive, because the Spirit who is the Spirit of spontaneity, who blows where He wills (John 3:8), is himself also the Spirit of Christ and therefore also the Spirit of truth (John 14:17). His business is to take what is Christ's and show it to us (John 16:15), and liturgy is one of the means by which in worship that mission is fulfilled. The Spirit who sets us free is also concerned with the framework; He also takes His bearings from the crucified and risen Lord. Equally, the Christ whose gospel requires the response of disciplined faithfulness is the Christ who came and died and rose to secure our freedom; to live within the framework of His truth is to be free indeed (John 8:36).

There is thus no possibility of conflict between Son and Spirit; the concern of both in their divine oneness is that within the framework of the Father's purposes we should retrieve our freedom. Charismatic spontaneity and liturgical conformity to the truth of Christ are not enemies, but allies in securing our well-ordered freedom. The task of the whole church in regard to its worship is to discover a new and creative relationship between liturgical tradition and charismatic liberation. Neither can be what God has called it to be without the other. At the moment, there is good hope that those whose worship has been centered in one are becoming more and more open to their need for the other and, most of all, to the Spirit of Christ in whom alone we shall be able to worship in Spirit and in truth.

SIX

The Rise of the Prophetic

NIGEL WRIGHT

━━━━

Once a movement adopts a promotional style and gains momentum, it must find energy from somewhere to keep going. It is no surprise, therefore, that the initiative headed by John Wimber and propagated all over the world through conferences should need to change tack from time to time by adding to its original message. Various notes have been struck over the last decade subsequent to the vision for signs and wonders, of which the most controversial has been the reemergence of the "prophetic." This is not an entirely new phenomenon. From 1979 onward David Pawson advanced a claim to fulfill a prophetic ministry. More recently Dr. Clifford Hill has argued, written, prophesied, and predicted along the same lines with the magazine *Prophecy Today*. What is new is the emergence of Paul Cain and the "Kansas City prophets," with an apparently advanced experience of this ministry.

John Wimber has described how in late 1988 he came into contact with Paul Cain and was stirred through him to a new level of concern for holiness and for the prophetic ministry, which until then he had not taken seriously.[1] Since that time this has been a major focus, and a merger of sorts has taken place between the Kansas City stream and the Vineyard. The emphasis has been propagated in conferences since July 1990. There are two aspects to the Kansas City phenomenon, the wider of which is associated with the name of Mike Bickle and takes a panoramic view of God's purposes in the next generation. It represents a form of post-millennialism often characteristic of enthusiastic movements. The narrower aspect, on which we intend to focus here, is expressed in the ministry of Paul Cain and takes the form of extended "words of knowledge." In meetings he identifies and addresses persons whom he normally does not know, by means of extensive knowledge of their circumstances. The utterances are astonishing in their accuracy.[2] Cain is a survivor from among the post-war healing evangelists, and has spent many years in virtual seclusion, only emerging relatively recently from the shadows. He gives every appearance of being a godly, vulnerable, and humble person. In recent months he has identified himself very closely with Dr. R. T. Kendall of the Westminster Chapel, London, to the extent of becoming a member of this church. This is a definite move to submit himself to the vigorous commitment to the teaching of Holy Scripture that Dr. Kendall represents.

Despite his gifts of knowledge, we may raise certain questions concerning Paul Cain's ministry. In October 1990 a series of meetings were held in this country that were preceded by the prophetic claim that revival would break out in London in October 1990. This claim was published by John Wimber with the words: "It has been prophesied by Paul Cain that revival will break out in Great Britain in October 1990. I am, by faith, believing that we will 'bring some back' to share in Anaheim at this event."[3] Wimber brought his whole family across to the UK to share in the projected event. It is evident in retrospect that this claim did not materialize in the way anticipated. Wimber himself has admitted to expecting far more, and that the outcome was a great disappointment.[4] At the same time, he seeks to exonerate Cain from blame by distinguishing between what was said and what he himself heard. When the prophecy is examined more closely, it turns out that Cain spoke only of "tokens" of revival as a prelude to something greater.[5] This in turn does not alleviate the problem, since it must still be decided what is meant by "revival" and by "tokens." To claim that there were tokens of revival in October 1990 does not appear to me to be substantiated by the evidence, but at this point the argument becomes subjective to the point of having to agree to differ. My personal judgment would be that not even this reduced version of the prophecy was fulfilled. Even if Wimber's reconstruction is accepted, it still leaves unanswered questions about why it is that Cain did not privately and publicly correct the false perception, especially when Wimber is portrayed as a close colleague of Cain and the two might be expected to discuss matters. It further begs the question as to what the value of contemporary prophecy might be if it is interpreted at the source in a way which changes its meaning.

Some elucidation might be gained by tracing Cain's antecedent, and by noting in particular his associations with the healing evangelist William Branham.[6] Similarities between the two may be noticed, including the frequency with which angels figure in their personal testimonies, and their astonishing accuracy in the "word of knowledge." Walter Hollenweger, a historian of Pentecostalism, acted as Branham's interpreter on visits to Switzerland, and records an interesting observation that whereas he was extremely accurate in diagnosing ailments, this was accompanied by "therapeutic failure," or lack of healing.[7] It appears that although a person is highly gifted in some areas, this does not mean they will be equally so in others, even where the expectation is that they might be. I suspect that something similar is true of Paul Cain. That he is gifted in the word of knowledge does not mean that when he ventures into wider prophetic utterances he is necessarily accurate at all. The mistake was to assume that his authority in one area would carry over into another. Cain may be better described as a "seer" than as a prophet, and this relativizes his significance without needing to label him as a false prophet. Like all of us, he is at his best when he sticks to his last.

Once more, in attempting to evaluate Cain's ministry we must consider the question of religious experience and the interaction of the spiritual and the psychic. If the analysis attempted elsewhere in this book stands (see Chapter 2), then we need to reckon with the psychic gifts which Cain possesses and with the streams of past religious experience by which he has been formed. To say that he is psychically gifted is in no way a criticism or condemnation, since the deeper question concerns the extent to which his natural humanity is being taken up, used, and extended by the Spirit of God to fulfil the purposes of God. The Spirit of God always comes incarnationally, that is, to fulfil His purposes *in* our humanity, not independently of it. But this perception also holds open the possibility that Cain may on occasion be displaying psychic aptitudes that are of no particular spiritual value.

Of greater concern would be the extent to which Cain is formed and shaped by the Branham stream of spiritual and religious experience. The fact that Branham slipped off into theological heterodoxy, and that his followers expected him to be raised from the dead after his accidental death, does not inspire confidence. Prophetic ability is apparently no guarantee of theological orthodoxy. Cain has in fact distanced himself from the doctrinal oddities associated with Branham, and this is reassuring. What is less clear is the extent to which someone may be shaped and formed by a religious movement at the subconscious levels, and the influence of that shaping remain, even though there is intentional distancing from it in formal terms. In short, what has rubbed off on Cain that not even he is aware of? And how are these factors to be brought to awareness and evaluated?

These speculative remarks lead us into a discussion about the nature and meaning of the prophetic in the contemporary church. It does not inspire confidence when we see claimants to the prophetic role engaged in the type of internal conflict that has been evidenced by the criticisms Clifford Hill levels against Cain and the Kansas City prophets. Hill took up the attacks of another charismatic Kansas City leader, Ernie Gruen, against the Kansas City prophets, and these were responded to in detail by Wimber.[8] Whatever the substance of the criticisms and their refutation, the controversy itself does not inspire us to believe that we are on secure ground, and it threatens to bring the whole notion of the prophetic into disrepute. The failure of the Cain prophecy concerning October 1990, or its interpretation in a misleading way, is a further destabilizing element in the discussion. The search is on, then, for a perspective on the prophetic which rings true.

The belief that God communicates with His people must be taken seriously, and is in fact fundamental to Christian living. Whether in the preached word, in guidance for the individual, or in the mind of the Church, it has traditionally been believed that God "speaks" to us, impresses a sense of His will upon us, and is the living God, not just the one who spoke in times past. In principle, there should be no great difficulty with accepting a prophetic dimension to our experience. This only sounds threatening when it is believed that the canonical role of Holy Scripture is being compromised. If it is understood that the Scriptures always remain normative, and yet need to be prophetically applied to our current circumstances, we may envisage a prophetic ministry that enhances rather than rivals the authority of revelation.

Such a prophetic ministry may be exercised in a variety of ways, and it is not the mode of delivery that determines what is prophetic and what is not, but the degree to which effective application is made to our lives and to the contemporary world. Because some insight is received without prior reflection, and with a heightening of the spiritual senses, does not mean that its content is any more prophetic than something which may be the product of careful thought and analysis. It is the matter which counts, not the form. Neither, conversely, does a high degree of subjectivity disqualify a word from being truly of God.

We may imagine various prophetic models. Martyn Lloyd-Jones and Martin Luther King both sought to apply the Word of God to the contemporary Church and society. Both did so with much thought and application, but also with intuitive instinct for what is right and appropriate. As prophetic models, they operated in a very different manner from Paul Cain, but in terms of their impact and force they are unlikely to be exceeded.

To make this point, it may be helpful to reflect upon these two figures, although it is stressed that they are being taken as representative characters only, and a similar exercise could be done in relation to many others. Martyn Lloyd-Jones was fundamentally an expository preacher in the Welsh tradition, occupying the pulpit at the Westminster Chapel in London in the post-war period. His style was unflamboyant, serious, and ponderous almost to the point of being dour. His method was that of thorough and exhaustive exposition of the biblical text, sometimes requiring years to complete a biblical book. As a gifted and, prior to his vocation to the ministry, a potentially distinguished physician, his diagnostic skills were outstanding. Applying them to the contemporary religious and secular scene, he was able to relate the biblical message as medicine to sickness with remarkable effectiveness. At the micro-level, his influence upon countless individuals, many future leaders among them—including leaders of the charismatic movement—was decisive and profound. At the macro-level, he made a strategic contribution to the development of the post-war Church, not least in the renewed interest in Puritan theology that has been a characteristic of some parts of it. In personality, Lloyd-Jones was the opposite of what might popularly be branded charismatic and prophetic. Yet accounts of his life make it plain that he was capable of penetrating inspirations as a counselor and preacher, through both prepared reflection and spontaneous intuition. As a voice to the Church, rooted in the knowledge of the Scriptures and in its own tradition, and as a figure who has influenced the shape of the contemporary Church, he must rank, in some considerable sense, as a prophetic figure, rediscovering the significance of the biblical revelation for the circumstances of the present.

Martin Luther King's prophetic qualities will be readily obvious to any student of modern history. He rose to prominence as a Baptist preacher born of Baptist preachers, and therefore steeped in the biblical story. His ministry was contextually specific in that he addressed the injustice of apartheid in the southern states of America, and yet it can be related to social injustice generally. His prophetic force was in both word and deed. His oratorical powers will live on as testimony to the power and force of the spoken word and of the biblical imagery of liberation and hope for the oppressed. Although backed with careful theological and social reflection (King was a well-qualified theologian), he had the ability to draw with profound inspiration upon his people's memory of the long history of injustice. The prophetic word was reinforced by prophetic actions as the freedom marches confronted the power structures of prejudice. Finally, he died the death of a prophet (it is certainly the case that in the Bible the life expectancy of prophets is not very high), and dying sealed the message of his life. There can be no doubt that King had grasped something fundamental about the revolutionary biblical word of freedom and the means of its realization in self-sacrifice.

It is not the intention of this exposition to diminish the contribution of Paul Cain by comparisons and contrasts, but rather to raise questions about the judgment with which we judge. It appears to me that by comparison with such models, however, Cain is more accurately described as a seer than a prophet, and that as such his gifts should be acknowledged and channeled.

But the contemporary Church has a decision to make and it involves careful theological, pastoral, and political reflection. What kind of prophetic ministry are we currently most in need of? While quite acknowl-

edging that the gifts represented by Cain are valuable, I have no hesi-
tation in asserting that those illustrated by Lloyd-Jones and King are
what we most of all need. This is not to elevate these figures unduly
since they too had their faults and partial perceptions, but to identify
what they brought to the mission of Christ.

A prophetic ministry that springs out of the exposition of the
Scriptures is less likely to become volatile and ensnared in mystical
subjectivism. A prophetic ministry that addresses the issues of an unjust
world is less likely to become in-house entertainment for the saints. For
the contemporary charismatic, there is the need to be willing to make
and stand by responsible theological judgments concerning what is good
for the mission of Christ, rather than to feel that because pronounce-
ments are made in an authoritative and subjective fashion they must
carry more weight. Discernment has as much to do with careful thought
and theological analysis as with inspired guesses and sudden intuitions.

SEVEN

Miracles As Holy:
The Spirituality of the Unexplained

ANDREW WALKER

On Miracles

It is clear that many modern theologians, following Bultmann, insist that miracles do not, by the nature of things, occur. Bultmann, deeply influenced by neo-Kantian philosophy and mechanistic physics, set up an antimony between the supernaturalism of the Bible and what he saw as the scientific world view: "It is impossible to use electric light and the wireless and to avail ourselves of modern medical and surgical discoveries, and at the same time to believe in the New Testament world of demons and spirits."[1]

While such a naturalistic view is in keeping with secular thought and a certain liberal habit of mind, it is impossible to square with the God of classical theology. Whether we like it or not, Christianity, according to the Fathers and the Reformers, rests upon a number of miraculous events that are constitutive of Christian faith. Without a belief, for example, in the incarnation and resurrection of our Lord—not to mention a God who creates the cosmos *ex nihilo*—Christianity has no objective foundations beyond experience and subjectivism. Furthermore, whatever some New Testament critics might say, no hermeneutic that pays serious attention to the beliefs of the gospel writers can doubt that they themselves were convinced that the Jesus of history was a miracle worker.

Interestingly, many Christians who accept the miracles of the New Testament deny the possibility that they also belong to the present. This holds not only for that phenomenon in Protestant evangelicalism known as dispensationalism, but also for many traditional Christians who feel uncomfortable at the thought that the Jesus of the New Testament might have the temerity to step out of the pages of the Bible and start working miracles in their living room or at the altar of their local church.

Charismatics stand against this view, and on the whole I stand with them for they have the logic of the gospels on their side. John 14:12, for example, does not say that the wonders of Christ will disappear with His passing. On the contrary, it says: "I tell you the truth, anyone who has faith in me will do what I have been doing. He will do even greater things than these, because I am going to the Father."

It is not, however, just a question of finding a text—and there are many more—to support the possibility of miracles beyond the apostolic era; there is evidence of church history to draw on, particularly in the lives of the saints in the Orthodox and Catholic traditions. It is also, if I may say so, a rather convenient apologetic to affirm the reality of miracles that are lost in the mists of history and are never subject to the tests of empirical enquiry!

Not that the miraculous sits comfortably in the realm of empirical investigation. My own dream experience, as recorded in Chapter 10, was of great existential importance to me—though, of course, it may not have been a miracle at all! But even if it was, it was not subject to empirical treatment, for there was nothing to observe—it was an event in my unconscious mind—and nobody but me experienced it.

Or again, Metropolitan Anthony tells of reading Mark's gospel and being aware of the presence of the living Christ. This experience was for him a real *metanoia* that changed his life, and those of us who know him or who have read his works can rightly say that we have evidence of a kind—by inference at least—that something happened to him, which had the nature of an encounter with the divine that is difficult to write off as a hallucination or as a delusion.

Indeed, in the realm of answered prayers many of us could attest to being assured that God had indeed led us, spoken to us, prompted us, or rebuked us, but we would not be able to provide empirical evidence for these convictions—the sort that would satisfy the rigors of natural science or the exactitude of laboratory experimentation.

It may very well be that we should preserve the word "miracle" for observable events in space and time, and separate these events from personal disclosures of God that are certainly meaningful to us but private and hence nonverifiable. When, however, claims are made that physical healings have taken place or that prophecies have been given that have been fulfilled, we have a duty to ensure that such claims are rigorously investigated, for they are events that are open both to falsification and verification.

We may object that empirical proof will not in itself convince an atheist or a humanist of the existence of the miraculous. The true skeptic, we might say, will always look for natural explanations of unexplained events, or substitute accounts of divine healing with plausible tales of spontaneous remission of diseases. However, empirical evidence can be decisive in matters of dispute. In the case of the Turin Shroud, for example, if radio-carbon dating had shown that the winding sheet was truly of first-century origin, then we would be left with only the possibility that it was the funeral shroud of our Lord. If, however, it showed that the shroud was hundreds of years later than the first century, then it would be a fake (as recent tests would seem to suggest).

On Investigating Miracles

It is precisely at the level of rigorous investigation into the miraculous that the Pentecostal movements, since their earliest days, have let themselves down. In the euphoria and excitement of revival, miracles have been testified to in abundance, but rarely verified. Testimonies are direct, successful, and personal means of communication, but they are by definition subjective and prone to exaggeration or capable of incorrect assessment. Congregations awash with the emotion of enthusiasm feed off rumor, conjecture, and hearsay. When you know that God heals, what you look for is not empirical evidence but tacit confirmation of your belief, in the form of positive reports, reconstructions of events, or books replete with amazing stories.

Sometimes something more sinister than credulity lies behind miraculous claims. Because miracles are crowd-pullers, charismatic Christianity can degenerate into a circus, with its mountebanks, frauds, and crowd-pleasers. Excited audiences at sea in a restless liturgy are malleable and vulnerable to the itinerant evangelists and peripatetic wonder-workers. There is power, sex, and money in Pentecostalism, as well as grace; if anyone doubts that, then the recent scandals of televangelism should be convincing enough.

However, chicanery is, in my opinion, rare. The Elmer Gantry character does exist, but delusions of grandeur, plain greed, and a hardening of the moral arteries accounts for more leadership scandals than overt fraud.

The creation of the "star" system, where the curious notion that the brilliant platform performer is somehow a saintly man of God, is partly to blame for the tawdry reputation of charismatic religion. But on the day-to-day level, what is more blatantly at fault is the lack of seriousness concerning the miraculous. What is needed is what we might call "quality control" of alleged charismata.

There are two reasons for this. The first reason is pragmatic. Silly and exaggerated claims bring the movement into disrepute. Nothing convinces people more that miracles do not occur than endless claims of bogus prophecies, unsubstantiated healings, and the sanctification of trivial supernatural happenings.

I remember as a teenager hearing a testimony of a lady who claimed that she was in bed late one night and could hear the steady drip drip of a tap. She decided to put her faith to the test and asked the dripping to stop in the name of Jesus. After prayer, she said, the dripping stopped. The testimony was greeted in our church with "Amens" and "Hallelujahs." I remember thinking, even as a committed Pentecostalist, *Why didn't she get up and turn off the tap herself?*

Today I still shudder at the "God found me a parking place" kind of testimony; it is not merely trite, it is unjust. Why should the charismatic Christian have a right to a parking space over someone else? In the light of Tom Smail's chapter on "The Cross and the Spirit," I think even this silliness exemplifies a spirituality that identifies more with power and privilege than the suffering servant of Calvary.

The second reason for insisting on quality control of miracles is more important than the first. Essentially, the substantiating of miraculous claims is a question of truth, and perhaps even of facing reality. I remember a house meeting in 1962 conducted by a well-known evangelist who insisted that the lady in front of us was healed of her long-standing disease. This was strange, because he was referring to her still *very* obvious goiter, a thyroid condition that causes a large swelling on the front of the throat. I had the evidence of my own eyes to go on, and was unimpressed with talk of the need for "the eyes of faith." The whole thing seemed to me just plain daft.

Dr. Peter May, who lives in Southampton in Hampshire, has been investigating healing since he was a medical student twenty years ago. He is an evangelical who is somewhat indifferent to the possibilities of modern miracles, but he remains passionate about calling a spade a spade and searching for the truth. His many case studies show reports of miracles that either fall under the category of hysteria and the psychosomatic (that is to say illnesses where there is no physical cause of disease), or claims (often made in good faith) that do not stand up to medical analysis.

He told me on one occasion that most people do not realize what is involved physiologically when claims are made that cancer has disappeared or that sight has been restored. In the case of the man with a withered arm who was healed by Jesus, he explained, we have to understand that in order for a man to "stretch out his hand," as the gospel account records, there had to be a reconnection of severed nerve ends and an instant replacement of lost muscle bulk.

So far, Dr. May has not found a single occurrence which he feels justifies the epithet "miracle." I share with him the conviction that often what pass as miracles are not shabby counterfeits, but fantasies. In my opinion, it only takes one miracle to stand up to scrutiny, one event that cannot be explained away by science or common sense, to change a person's world view and open them to the possibility of faith.

Physical Phenomena As Miracles

Too often, I believe, we have confused the miraculous with observed behavioral phenomena. During the dramatized documentary of the life of Edward Irving on BBC radio in 1984, Professor T. F. Torrance made the telling remark that Irving confused the spiritual with the phenomenal. Now there are two ways to read this. Either we can say that the spiritual will have no demonstrable phenomenal effect, or we can say that phenomena in themselves do not necessarily entail anything of spiritual significance.

I prefer the second view, for I feel that the first possibility is anti-materialist. It seems to me quite logical that in a material universe spiritual activity will sometimes have an observable physical effect. So, for example, during the Great Awakening in North America in the eighteenth century, Jonathan Edwards was able both to be in the thick of the revival and to stand back and scientifically analyze his wife's "religious affections." The Wimber thesis, that natural physical predis-positions will play a part in "signs and wonders," also seems to me to be a right and proper response to spiritual realities.

This is a two-edged sword, however, because shaking, sighing, bark-ing, screaming, falling over, going into a trance, feelings of ecstasy, and "transports of delight" do not in themselves indicate anything miracu-lous. Charismatic meetings are replete with these phenomena. Admit-tedly, they are also augmented by tongues, prophecies, words of knowl-edge, etc. These in themselves, for many believers, are evidence of the Spirit's power. In an article I coauthored twenty years ago,[2] I talked of what I called a "time of blessing," when the very fact that God was experienced as present in the tongues and the prophecies seemed to be more important to the believers than the actual messages decoded from the *glossolalia* or heard through the natural language of prophetic utter-ance. In other words, what seemed to be of crucial significance to the congregation was *that* God spoke, not *what* He actually said.

Nigel Wright has suggested in his book that what we often call supernatural events may sometimes be psychic (natural) phenomena that may or may not be of God's Spirit.[3] This sensible approach avoids both psychological reductionism and over-spiritualizing the natural world. I endorse such a view, but would make a plea that we do not underestimate the possibility that sometimes physical phenomena are neither miraculous nor natural forces: they are psycho-social construc-tions. When, for example, you have a large audience together under the direction of charismatic personalities (using "charismatic" in the popular, secular sense), you are involved in what we might call the group dy-namics of the crowd. This is not to make odious comparisons between the rallies of Billy Graham and Hitler—or a Michael Jackson pop con-cert, for that matter—but it is to point out that large audiences are receptive to platform cues and crowd happenings.

What is so very different, phenomenologically, from the audience response to the evangelist of being "slain in the Spirit," and the responses to the suggestions of mass hypnotists on a carnival pier in the summer season? The power of suggestion in an atmosphere of excitement is stronger than one might suppose.

Doing what other people are doing is contagious in crowds. Not only does crowd behavior follow an inner dynamic of its own, it is subject to the dominance of the partisan. Witness the antics of football supporters with their ritualistic gestures of defiance and disdain. Watch the lifted arms and swaying torsos of joyous believers at Spring Harvest. Hear the rattle of spears on shields as tribal warriors prepare for battle.

Crowds also capitulate to fashion. Once girls started to throw their knickers at the singer Tom Jones, it became a regular feature of his shows. In 1991 the "Mexican wave" arrived on the center court at Wimbledon! Once words of knowledge appeared on the charismatic scene, they became *de rigueur* in the renewal and the so-called "new churches."

There are other issues that go beyond the dynamics of crowd behavior. Are words of knowledge really direct messages from God, statistical probabilities (given the large numbers of people present), or, more loosely, simply hit-and-miss affairs? Who checks the correlation between words of knowledge, which in the case of healings are taken to be an accurate form of diagnosis, and successful healing rates? In a large congregation, where excitable behavioral patterns are set and expectations that God will heal are high, the chances are slim that there will be a careful assessment of results.

All these observations and enquiries may seem to be negative and cynical, but in upholding a belief in miracles nothing short of total integrity in dealing with them will do. Fervently to believe in them surely entails the moral imperative to protect them from fraudulence or from frivolity and shoddiness. This is, in my opinion, more than an empirical issue: it is a question of holiness.

Miracles As Holy

Holiness underlies the Orthodox attitude to the sacraments: "holy things to those that are holy," insists the liturgy of St. John Chrysostom. Again, when the gospel is brought from the sanctuary into the main body of the church, it is held high for the congregation to reverence: as the priest reads, the people stop their chattering, cross themselves, and give heed to the Scripture, for it is God who is speaking.

The presence of God provokes wonder. As Rudolph Otto put it, the experience of the numinous necessitates awe: it is in itself a marvel. We think of Moses and the burning bush, and how in the face of God's theophany the great leader was compelled to remove his shoes. The miracle was not the phenomenon of the unconsumed bush *per se*: it was the visible reality of God's marvelous presence—a presence which was so overwhelming that the very ground in its synergy with the divine life was hallowed. On the Mount of Transfiguration the disciples were, in a way, reminiscent of Moses, overcome by the Shekinah glory, the "uncreated light" of God, "and they were greatly afraid." These stories indicate to us that God is not the author of party tricks or shamanite shenanigans: He is the Holy One—the Ancient of Days. We prefix the word Trinity with Holy to indicate the sacred and sanctified nature of God. When we pray, "Our Father, hallowed be thy name . . . ," we are beginning with a recognition of holiness as a primary attribute of the godhead.

If all this sounds rather grand and mysterious, so much the better; for a miracle is either God with us in a remarkable and marvelous way, or it is nothing at all. A miracle may conceivably lead us to fall over, but it should certainly impel us to cry out for mercy. When overcome by the nearness of God, or in the presence of the "holy mysteries," the Eastern Orthodox find it most natural to prostrate themselves. This may be less natural for those of us who are Occidentals, but through their body language Orthodox believers demonstrate what is, I believe, always the appropriate response to the miraculous—wonder, and what we should not be ashamed of calling holy fear.

Holiness instills sobriety into our worship and invests stillness into the heart of our liturgies. It teaches us that to be lost in praise is more than settling for a frenetic jolliness. Holiness leads from a shift in focus from our feelings about God to God himself; from the gifts of the Spirit to the Spirit as the Holy Giver of the gifts; from being slain in the Spirit to offering ourselves as an offering to be "slain"—"Though he slay me, yet will I hope in him" (Job 13:15).

An understanding of the miraculous as holy will not lead to a denial of the gifts, but it will probably lead to a noticeable drop in the number of reported healings and discarding of the many trivial pursuits that clutter our worship. For, when the Holy Spirit comes, He will lead us into all truth and separate the wheat of divine grace from the chaff of human folly.

THREE

Experiencing the Renewal

EIGHT
A Renewal Recalled
TOM SMAIL

I say "recalled" rather than "remembered" because to remember is to cast the mind back to past events that are over, whereas to recall is to recognize the continuing activity and power of these past events in the present day. So in what follows, I do not merely remember my personal experience of renewal in the Holy Spirit as something that happened in the middle of November 1965, but from which I am now separated by the passing of more than twenty-five years; rather, I recall it as something that indeed started then but has never finished, so that it does not belong to the past but continues to mold and shape me, as I live and work in a quite different context and as a much older man.

What I have to say now is not exactly what I would have said about it then. What I said then came out of the fresh and almost overwhelming immediacy of the experience itself in all its wonderful and transforming newness and self-evident simplicity, without perhaps too much awareness of all the complicated questions it was going to raise for me in particular and for the Church in general. In what I say now the exuberant thanksgiving has, perhaps inevitably, given way to a much more tranquil and reflective thankfulness. This may be a good deal less exhilarating, but has the compensating advantage of letting me see what happened not just as a personally exciting experience but in the wider context of what led up to it and what followed from it. In the intervening years I have had time and opportunity to appreciate how what God did in me then relates to other aspects of His dealings with me through Christ in the Spirit, some of which preceded and some of which has come after the experience of renewal.

These early days were something of a charismatic honeymoon during which I gave most of my attention to exploring and rejoicing in the wonderful new thing that I had been given; but charismatic honeymoons, like all others, have to end and the new thing has to be brought home and find its place among all the other God-given gifts that constitute our life in Christ.

Of course, if the honeymoon immediately follows the marriage, the wooing, which may take a long time, precedes it. The Holy Spirit was ready for me long before I was ready for Him, and the renewal experience had before it a long process during which I was gradually made aware both of what the Spirit could do and of my own need, both as man and as minister, for Him to do it in and through me. One of the reasons why nowadays I avoid describing a renewal experience as "baptism in the Spirit" is that baptism speaks of birth and beginning, the coming into a life of something that was not there before. The Holy Spirit was in my life long before 1965, long before I had any formulated awareness of charismatic experiences and gifts, as indeed according to Paul He is at work in the lives of all Christians who confess Jesus as Lord (1 Corinthians 12:3), quite irrespective of their attitude to and experience of things charismatic. In my own case I had to be led firmly but gently in the charismatic direction over quite a few years, and the Holy Spirit was as active in one way when He was leading to the renewal experience as He was active in another way within the experience itself.

On the face of it I was a very unlikely candidate for charismatic renewal—a young Scottish Presbyterian minister who, both by my ecclesiastical tradition and temperament, was unsympathetic toward, and even afraid of, the unsystematic spontaneity and emotional abandon of Pentecostal Christianity. What mattered most to me was the Word rather than the Spirit, the correctness of the theology rather than the exuberance of the praise, the preparedness and penetration of the preaching rather than the depth of the response to it, the good ordering of the body of Christ for its work and witness rather than the giftedness of its various members. Furthermore, the theology of Karl Barth and T. F. Torrance that had shaped me most then, and is still very important to me, tended to reinforce my own suspicions and disinclinations about more Pentecostal responses to the gospel.

All in all I was a pretty tough nut for the Spirit to crack, but it belongs to His grace that He can see the need underneath the resistance, and He will set himself to a gentle but persistent wooing of the most reluctant and resistant Christian. I first became aware of the more charismatic dimensions of His activity a good ten years before my personal renewal in relation to a pastoral situation in my first parish with which nothing in my sophisticated reformed theology had equipped me to cope.

A middle-aged lady, who was a member of my congregation, had been diagnosed as having an inoperable cancer of the esophagus and had been sent home to die in a condition that had reduced her to little more than an emaciated bundle of yellowing skin and bone, deeply distressing to her and all who cared for her. Like most clergy I felt totally helpless, but at the same time unwilling simply to let matters take their course. Apart from minimal contact with the pioneering healing ministry of Rev. Cameron Peddie, I knew almost nothing about Christian healing, let alone charismatic gifts, but, more in desperation than inspiration, I suggested to the sick woman's husband that I might come in each Thursday afternoon and pray with her.

I remember it as a pretty low-key exercise—short opening prayer, laying on of hands, short concluding blessing, and departure. But after six or seven weeks of this she was recalled to the hospital and X-rayed, with the quite unexpected and to us amazing result that the cancer had shrunk and that an operation for its removal was now feasible. A long surgical process followed, during which the diseased esophagus was replaced by a new artificial one. It took the doctors to complete what God had started, but the result was that she was completely restored to normal weight and health and lived a full life for many years afterward.

The family and I, along with those in the church who knew the situation, were both astounded and full of joy, and her own relationship to God was completely transformed. The God that we spent so much time reading and talking about had actually taken a hand in our lives at a crucial point; the rescuing grace that had been the subject of sermons had acted unexpectedly and decisively before our very eyes—not because we were full of faith and expectation (we had very little of either), but because we had confessed our impotence and had thrown ourselves on the mercy of God and He had answered our cry. The biblical verse that is the key to that healing and to much renewal is Peter's quotation from Joel 3 in his Pentecost sermon in Acts 2:21, "Everyone who calls on the name of the Lord will be saved." For all our lack of faith and expectancy, we had called upon the name of the Lord and He had done for us by His Spirit much more than we had dared to ask.

I am quite sure that verse contains the recipe for all Christian renewal, which comes, not in response to complicated and esoteric techniques, but simply by turning from our own efforts to do God's work for Him and throwing ourselves on His mercy and His promises to do for us and in us by His Spirit what we cannot do by ourselves for Him.

That was clearly exemplified in the healing I have been describing, but although I rejoiced in what had happened it was a good few years before I came to terms with what it was saying to me. By that time I was minister of a large and active congregation at the heart of industrial Scotland, with a full church on Sundays and a bewildering array of activities of all kinds during the week. But renewal is needed often as much when churches are full and busy as when they are empty and lethargic. In that situation I found myself increasingly frustrated and disappointed, because, for all our numbers and good works, there seemed to be only a few signs that the gospel I preached every Sunday was proving itself effective in the lives of those who heard it, and that frustration was soon to be brought to a head in a quite dramatic way.

About two miles along the road from us there was a new small church about which strange stories began to circulate. The minister and some of its members were saying that they had been filled with the Holy Spirit and were beginning to exercise some of the spiritual gifts listed in 1 Corinthians 12 and were indeed holding meetings in which they spoke in tongues. When this began to be reported in the tabloid press, we who were their near neighbors had to take notice and make some response.

Predictably, that response was pretty negative, and perhaps even a little patronizing as well. I can remember preaching a sermon in which I said that dramatic charismatic phenomena like the ones we had been hearing about among our neighbors were no doubt very fascinating but they were really quite unimportant. Whether or not you had any of the spiritual gifts that Paul lists and discusses in 1 Corinthians 12 and 14 did not matter very much provided you had the love that he extols in Chapter 13. We in our church might not have many of the gifts, but we had quite a lot of the love, and that in the end was what counted. I do not know quite how I would have responded if anybody had drawn my attention to the first verse of Chapter 14, where far from making spiritual gifts and love mutually exclusive alternatives, as I was doing, Paul tells us that we need them both and should be greatly concerned to exercise them both: "Follow the way of love *and eagerly desire spiritual gifts*, especially the gift of prophecy."

I sometimes advise my fellow preachers that they need to be very careful about what they say in sermons because, although the congregation may not be paying attention, the good Lord most certainly is. In my sermon I had more or less dismissed the charismatic gifts by saying that because we had love we did not need them. Over the next months circumstances unexpectedly conspired to demonstrate both to the preacher and the hearers of that sermon just how little love we in fact had.

Over the winter of 1964–65 we became embroiled in one of those unhappy and bitter internal conflicts that afflict most churches at one time or another and in the midst of which many people are deeply wounded and hurt. Sunday schools and choirs are often the septic foci from which the divisive and debilitating poison can spread through the whole body of a congregation, threatening its unity, dulling its worship, diverting the energies it should be devoting to the concerns of Christ's kingdom.

It was such a situation that we had to contend with. There is no need to rehearse the details, save to say that it showed us that, with a few glorious exceptions, most of us, when our relationships were put to the test, did not have the quality of love to face the difficult situation and pray and work for a way to deal with it in a creative rather than a destructive way.

It all dragged on for months, and by the time it ended with a final showdown, the frustration that I had been feeling before it started had turned into a considerable depression, so that it took tranquilizers by day and sleeping tablets at night to keep me going at all, and the signs were appearing that I might be on the way to a complete breakdown.

I can remember during the quieter summer months of 1965 thinking dark thoughts about getting out of the ministry, feeling utterly disappointed at what had happened, and the inability of the congregation to deal with it in the light of the gospel I had been preaching to them, with a deep feeling of personal failure that not only had I been unable to lead others through, but had myself all but collapsed under the onslaught.

Many ministers in many different churches over recent years will have felt exactly the same. Some have left, some have slogged on without much hope or expectation that anything will ever be any different, but for many the collapse of confidence in the church, and most of all in themselves, has been the preliminary to a new and very serious turning back to God to see if, where our resources have been routed, His resources can rescue us from the messes we have made and get us on our feet again in hope and in strength to contend and prevail. Sometimes God has to pull all the carpets out from under our feet, because it is only when we are flat on our backs, with our self-sufficiency shattered, that we will at last begin to look upward to Him.

In my own case, it was that summer, in the dull calm after the calamitous storm, that God began to show His hand again. One of the key couples in the congregation came back from a summer holiday with the Iona Community, saying that they had met a young minister from one of Glasgow's most deprived areas, who told them that he and some members of his congregation had been renewed by the Holy Spirit. My couple rather diffidently told me the outlines of his story, which had obviously affected them deeply, and added, "Of course we know that is not the sort of thing that you would be interested in."

Everything they knew about me up to that time fully justified that comment. But now I was on my spiritual beam ends and I knew that if anybody was offering a new beginning in the name of Christ, neither I personally nor my people could afford not to listen and to consider seriously what he had to say. So I invited the minister from Glasgow to come and speak to us one Sunday evening and asked people to stay on after the service to hear his story; some forty did. Our reaction was mixed but very significant. On the one hand we were very disappointed; he was a diffident speaker, neither very articulate nor coherent, so that to listen was quite difficult. On the other hand, precisely because he was like that, there came through his unimpressive presentation a great sense of the reality of what he was talking about. To use Pauline language, the earthiness of the vessel enhanced by contrast the transcendent value of the treasure that had been deposited in it, and quite a few of us who heard him knew that we could not just go home and do nothing at the end of the meeting. We felt we were being pointed to something big that we needed but that up till now we had not been able to find. So about twelve of us, at that point nearly all women, agreed to go on meeting every Sunday evening to study all the main New Testament passages about the Holy Spirit and pray for His coming.

This we did for about six or seven weeks, and made very little obvious progress. We did not know how to cope with the Bible in a group situation, and very few of us had the confidence to pray aloud. Sometimes you have to be bored together before you can be blessed together, and we were often quite bored on these autumn Sunday evenings. Nevertheless we persisted, because we had the mostly unspoken sense that we were on to something of great importance that would give itself to us in its own time and its own way. Till it did, we waited with what patience and hope we could muster and wondered when and from what direction the new move would come.

It came in the month of November and through a man called Denis Bennett, an American Episcopalian priest who had been renewed by the Holy Spirit, forced out of his parish as a result, and was touring Britain under the auspices of the newly formed Fountain Trust. It was announced that he was coming to our town to hold a meeting for ministers in the afternoon and an open meeting for everybody in the evening. In our Sunday group it was agreed that I would go to the former and the others to the latter.

I arrived late at the ministers' meeting, a sign of my reluctance to expose myself to what I thought the main burden of the message was going to be. I had stereotyped Bennett as the kind of evangelical revivalist who would tell us all how wicked we were and exhort us to repent and turn back to God. Apart from the many sophisticated theological objections I had to such an approach, in my condition at that time I just could not cope with it. I knew I was in a mess, and did not need to have that rubbed in anymore, and I just did not have what it took to respond to any demand for repentance that might be made of me. What I needed to know at that moment was not what God required of me, but what He was willing to do for me; not the demands of His law, but the free generosity of His grace.

To my complete surprise a story about the free generosity of God in the pouring out of His Spirit was exactly what I was offered that memorable afternoon. The content of Bennett's talk was soon after published under the title *Nine O'Clock in the Morning*, a book that is still in print and that has been the gateway to personal renewal for very many people down the years.

What came over me that day was the joy of the man and the sense of immediacy and firsthand reality as he described what God had done for him by His Spirit. He had been through the same sort of bitter ecclesiastical in-fighting as me, but he had not been embittered or brought down by it as I had, and he was able to give many examples of the difference that the new filling of the Spirit had made to his life and ministry, some of which reminded me of the healing in my first parish ten years before. The difference was that for me that had been a one-time wonder, whereas for him it was part of his regular expectation of what the living God would do when His Spirit was free to move among us.

If I was last in to that meeting, I was also the first out. Bennett offered to talk and pray with anyone who wanted to, but I did not want to talk to anybody until I had gotten things sorted out a little in my own mind. As I drove home, two competing reactions to what I had heard struggled within me. On the one hand the theologian in me told me that Bennett's theology was impossible. He seemed to have swallowed classical Pentecosalism quite uncritically. He spoke of what he called "the baptism in the Holy Spirit" as a second blessing that came to those who had fulfilled the conditions for receiving it and whose invariable authenticating evidence was speaking in tongues. I knew that with my reformed background and convictions I could never speak in these terms, and, as Chapter 1 of this book shows, I have ever since been trying to work out a theology of renewal that would do justice to essential Pentecostal insights but would integrate them into the whole range of gospel truth in a more adequate way.

It would therefore have been easy for me to get out my sharp Barthian scissors, to cut up into little pieces all that Bennett had said, and to dismiss it on the grounds of its doctrinal unacceptability and theological inadequacy. What stopped me from doing that was the sheer fact that I could not ignore that, for all my vaunted theological correctness, Bennett was moving in a dimension of joyful relationship to God and experience of His presence, power, and promises, whereas I was struggling with failure and incapacity and it was taking me all my time to keep going at all.

So what was I to do? The answer was both simple and crucial, and it is the clue to all authentic Christian renewal. It can be stated in three words, but its consequences will fill more than a lifetime: seek God himself. The heart of personal renewal is not in thinking about God, talking about God, or undertaking and organizing worthy enterprises in the service of the kingdom of God; it is in opening yourself up to God. It means turning from all the things that you have been doing for Him, to ask Him what only He can do, and breathe His life and energy into you. To learn that was to apply in a much wider context the lesson I had partly learned from the healing: "Everyone who calls on the name of the Lord will be saved."

The theological enterprise that mattered so much to me, and still does, is secondary to that, because how can you know what to say about God if you do not know the God of whom you are speaking? And how can you serve Him and His kingdom if you are not in touch with the King you claim to be serving and lack the spiritual energy to fulfil His purposes, once you have discovered them? These were the questions I asked myself on that drive home from the Bennett meeting that day, and by the time I reached my journey's end I was echoing the words of the psalmist: "O God, you are my God, earnestly I seek you; my soul thirsts for you, my body longs for you, in a dry and weary land where there is no water" (Psalm 63:1).

In the goodness of God I did not have long to wait for the answer to that prayer. In three memorable weeks in November 1965, in the only major religious crisis I have ever experienced, my spiritual condition and my relationship to God were dramatically transformed, to such an extent that the family and the congregation began to notice the difference and to wonder what was happening. It was not a change from unbelief to faith, or in the content of what I believed. The faith I had believed from my earliest years up I believed still. There were those around at the time who, for their own reasons, tried to persuade me that what had happened was some kind of evangelical conversion, but to see it in that way would have been to slander the genuine work that God had already done in my life, when He drew me to trust Christ and called me to the ministry of the gospel that had Christ at its center.

It was not a coming to faith, but rather a personal entering into the good of what I had always believed. What I had always taught others that the living Christ could do for them, I now found Him doing for me in a deeper and more radical way than ever before. So it had to do with the Holy Spirit, because it is precisely the business of the Holy Spirit to "take . . . what is mine and make it known to you" (John 16:15). Or, to put it in Pauline terms, it is by the Spirit that we are "changed into [Christ's] likeness from one degree of glory to another" (2 Corinthians 3:18, RSV). What the Holy Spirit was doing was to take what I had always affirmed of Jesus and make some of it actually happen in me, so that at least to some degree my experience of God began to reflect His, the way a mirror reflects the object at which it is directed. I can make these general statements much more specific by describing four different facets of my renewal that were inextricably bound up together.

First, it was a renewal in my relationship to God. Jesus knew God intimately as His Father, and opened the way for us to do the same, and it is specifically the mission of the Spirit to cry "*Abba*, Father" in our hearts (Galatians 4:6). In these November weeks a prayer life that had been at best dutiful and at worst non-existent suddenly flowered into a most intimate and overwhelmingly joyful contact with the living God and His Son, so that I was almost afraid to go into the room and shut the door for the intensity of the self-abandoning absorption in God's goodness and grace that kept on being given to me. All the sadness and disappointment of the previous months were swept away in the sense of His nearness and all the hope for the future that it brought with it. I could not open my Bible without being personally and relevantly addressed from its pages; I could not kneel down to pray without the sense of His gracious presence, ready to hear, fast to answer.

To begin with, my Barthian suspicion of mystical experience made me hold back, but this was no contentless mysticism, no pantheistic absorption into a faceless Beyond. The Spirit who led me into it was the Spirit who confesses the lordship of Jesus Christ, and the communion into which He brought me was quite specifically with the crucified, risen, and ascended Lord: it was in Him, His presence, His pardon, His promises, His undeserved grace, that I rejoiced.

Of course that intimate intensity in prayer did not continue indefinitely, and it was in fact somewhat of a relief when it began to recede a little. I have my dull patches and my difficulties in praying, like everybody else, but that special time had done its work; living contact with God was reestablished, and what was given in those days has never been withdrawn. When I am dull to seek God and when God is slow to answer me, I recall what He gave me then and know that I live still in the same grace that in its own time and its own way will still hear and answer.

Second, the new closeness with God resulted in a new closeness with other people. At the time of my renewal I was involved in a series of one-to-one interviews with some teenage young people who were about to be confirmed. It was a task I always dreaded because it was very hard to break through their reticence and my own, to have any meaningful exchanges on a spiritual level. But this time it was amazingly different. Not that I did anything different, but, to my great surprise, one after the other the youngsters began to open up to me quite spontaneously and tell me where they really stood on the great issues of faith and discipleship, so that there was great discontent in the waiting-room as interviews that were scheduled for fifteen minutes ran to half an hour or more as we talked together about what it meant to believe the gospel and follow the Lord.

What had changed to make that possible? I sometimes say that it was the smell! People have a nose for love; where it is absent they clam up, where it is present they open up. For, again according to Paul, "God has poured out his love into our hearts by the Holy Spirit, whom he has given us" (Romans 5:5). I am not by temperament the most outgoing of men, but I can only surmise that my own personal reception of the outpouring of the Spirit had made me smell a little of God's kind of accepting love, that the young folk coming in had sensed some of that, that it overcame the gaps of age, status, and temperament between us and made them at ease enough to speak freely to me. He is the reconciling Spirit, the ecumenical Spirit, the uniting Spirit who takes the peace that Christ's love for the world made on the cross and works it into us, so as to transform our relationships with those around us. As surely as He is the Spirit of the first great commandment who enables us to start loving the Lord our God with at least some of our heart and mind and soul and strength, He is also the Spirit of the second great command, who breaks through our isolation and alienation from one another and shows us at least sometimes what it is like to love our neighbor as ourselves.

Third, He is the sanctifying Spirit who gives us a taste of victory in the moral struggle with ourselves. At the time of my renewal, there was something in my life that I knew was wrong and destructive but could not overcome. My good intentions, resolutions, and strenuous efforts had failed to deal with it in any lasting way and it haunted me all the time from the shadows, a hidden reproach of guilt and failure. With the fresh coming of the Spirit all that was changed; in a way that I did not understand, the furniture of my subconscious self was moved around, so that for quite a long time what had been a constant source of temptation did not trouble me at all. Since then, on that same battle-field the fight had been resumed and there have been both defeats and victories, but the whole situation has looked different since then, because I have discovered that God's grace is greater than my sin, and our sins are not just forgiven but in the Spirit can be overcome. "Jesus saves" is not just a biblical slogan or a hope for heaven, but a reality that can at least in part be experienced here and now today.

In my renewal I encountered in a new way the Spirit of prayer, the Spirit of love, and the Spirit of victory: He gave me a taste of transformation in my relationship to God, to other people, and to myself. That for me was and is the heart of renewal, and you will notice that as yet I have not mentioned at all the whole dimension of charismatic gifts. For others that has been central, for me it was always somewhat peripheral. It followed the rest, as I shall describe, and it is a dimension in which by God's grace I from time to time still operate, sometimes with wonder and gratitude at what He does through me. There were and there are gifts to pray for and receive, but even if there had been no gifts, there would still have been renewal; even if I had now known

136

anything of tongues, prophecy, and healing, I would still have been renewed by the Spirit, because He brought me closer to God and to people and made me a bit more free in dealing with myself, and in that there is more than enough for joy and for praise.

However, the gifts were also added. I believe nowadays that the gifts become significant and escape from ambiguity and banality when those who receive them have been brought by the Spirit into close relationship with God and their neighbors and are in good command of themselves. Where we are not sanctified in these three relationships, the gifts themselves can become vehicles of arrogance, self-assertion, and division rather than testimonies to grace, love, and peace. Spiritual gifts are dangerous in the hands of fleshy people, as Paul's warnings to the Corinthians clearly show. On the other hand, when the gifts of the Spirit come to people who are in the freshness and reality of the Spirit, the possibilities are open and endless.

In 1965, in the midst of my renewal, spiritual gifts were at first still largely beyond my knowing. Then one night, when I was washing my face, making ready for bed, some strange syllables and unknown words came unbidden into my head. My first reaction was to give myself a good shake and dismiss the whole thing from my mind, but it proved too insistent for that. Next day, driving home from some hospital visiting, it happened again. My reaction this time was not to dismiss the strange words, but to say to myself, "Whether this is me or God I do now know, but whatever it is, I shall offer it up to Him and praise Him with it, and that cannot be wrong." So there and then in the car I started to sing in tongues, and, as I sang, a bit of me deep down that had been bottled up began to be set free. It was as if someone had pulled out the cork from the rich wine and the champagne came bubbling to the surface in God's praise. It was exactly what I needed at that time to complement all the other things that the Spirit was doing in me. My relationship with God needed to be widened out from its far too cerebral expression; it needed to escape from idea into emotion, from thought into enthusiasm, from credal prose into worshiping song, and for me the gift of tongues was one very significant way in which that could happen.

I use that gift only infrequently nowadays, more often in times of perplexity than at moments of exultation. I have never thought or believed that speaking in tongues was the necessary evidence of being renewed in the Spirit, but I do believe on the basis of my own experience that for some people at some times it is a releasing and renewing gift from God, and think of it as a part of my prayer equipment that is available when it is required. Other gifts followed—in my case prophecy, sometimes quite specific and relevant to particular people and situations; and a little healing, very occasionally of a dramatic kind, although, to keep the record straight, I must add that sometimes the prophecies have been quite wrong-headed and often there has been no observable response to the ministry of healing. My experience in the whole realm of gifts convinces me that cynical dismissal and uncritical affirmation are both inappropriate responses to it. There are more genuine manifestations of the Spirit than evangelical and radical opponents will admit, but fewer than many overcredulous charismatics claim.

When the New Testament writers deal with spiritual gifts, they often underline the need for the exercise of discernment, to distinguish the good from the bad, what is divine gift from what is human invention, what is genuine from what is imaginary (cf. 1 Corinthians 12:10; 1 Thessalonians 5:19–22; 1 John 4:1–3). The gift of discernment has been somewhat neglected in some contemporary charismatic circles, but it is perhaps the gift that most of all needs to be sought and cultivated, because its exercise is the key to the right use of all the rest.

My extended exposition of my renewal experience has perhaps shrouded the dramatic effect that it had on me at the time. I felt a quite different man at the end of November 1965 than I did at the beginning, and I knew that the difference owed nothing at all to my achievement but everything to the gracious activity of the Holy Spirit of God. He had given me prayer, He had given me love, He had given me victory, and He had begun to show me that His grace could become very specific and concrete in the various gifts that I had begun to exercise. All this was a sign that God was accepting, affirming, and renewing me and my ministry at a time when I was feeling more than a little hopeless about both. To recall that affirmation, and to find that it was constantly being reaffirmed in all sorts of situations where the going was very hard has been one of my chief sources of strength from that day to this.

To know that God is affirming you not just in gospel word but in the experienced eventfulness of His Spirit within you and around you sets you free both from dependence on the good opinions of other people and from the substitute means of support that come out of packets and bottles. Almost immediately after my renewal experience the tranquillizers and the sleeping pills were flushed away, because they were no longer needed. Of course there are times and conditions when these things have their proper use, and when I would use them, but they will not serve as adequate substitutes for the life and joy that God's Spirit brings.

I have told a little of the start of my own renewal, but what I have said is out of its proper context, because I have not had space to tell you what was happening to my wife and those around me at the same time, and what subsequently happened in the life of the congregation to which we all belonged. My renewal began when I went to Denis Bennett's meeting for minsters in the afternoon, theirs when they went the same evening. All that followed for us and for the church depended on the fact that what God had given us drew us together in a new way that had effects far beyond our own little circle. That must remain for now another story, but it is good to remember that, although Pentecost is personal, it is never individual. The Spirit is given not just to renew individual church members but the whole corporate body to which they belong, so that that body can be commissioned and empowered to proclaim the word of the gospel that in the power of the Spirit can set up signs, foretastes, and promises of Christ's kingdom in every aspect of the world's life.

In order to be renewed, I had, as I have explained, placed a temporary moratorium on my theological activity. But now that I knew for myself the reality of the Spirit I had seen at work in Denis Bennett, I had to take up the challenge of trying to understand it in a way that was quite different from his. The understanding could not precede the experience, but it did have to follow it; how that understanding had developed at one of its central points, my first more theological contribution to this book has tried to make clear.

NINE
A Pilgrimage in Renewal
NIGEL WRIGHT

———

As they say, life must be lived forward but it can only be understood backward. At the time, and looking forward, it feels to be the case that one is steering one's own ship and that each decision is deliberately and self-consciously taken. In retrospect, it appears rather that one has been carried along by a tide of events and circumstances, that the room for maneuver was never great in the first place, and that most decisions were more or less inevitable. This is now how I see things, not in a fatalistic way, but in the sense that there is a providence which shapes our ends.

To say that I was born in 1949 places me decisively in the post-war baby boom. It also means that I came to consciousness in the 1960s and am a product of that decade. The large and self-respecting family into which I was born as the youngest child was a product of northern artisan culture fused with a somewhat more aristocratic Scottish line of descent. In religious terms we were post-Christian and post-nonconformist. On my father's side, the ancestry was Methodist, Liberal, and Cooperative Society in orientation. My mother's side was always more obscure, but the nonconformist heritage was there also. The last two generations had been Salvation Army, with my parents being brought up and having married in this tradition. However, disillusionment had set in prior to the war and they had moved first to the Quakers and then for almost a year to become members of an exiled German religious community known as the Bruderhof, the Society of Brothers. At the beginning of the war this was a very risky thing to do. Having been harried out of Nazi Germany, this neo-Hutterite community had taken refuge in England and gathered some British adherents, my own family among them. In the event, because of lack of religious agreement, things did not work out, and in 1940 my father, leaving aside his pacifist views, made the transition via the Labour Corps into war service and officer-ship in the Royal Engineers while the rest of the family settled down for the duration in Cheshire and then, in 1944, in darkest Manchester.

It was here that I saw the light of day and had my first experiences. They did not include the active practice of any religious faith. None-theless, the echoes of a faith were there in the background—an uncle and aunt who were brigadiers in the Salvation Army, a general and sincere respect for genuinely committed Christian people and corre-sponding contempt for religious show and hypocrisy, and instinctive cultural Protestantism and a living, though nonreligious, nonconformity. Andrew Walker on one occasion referred to those who once they give up being Christians do not cease to be Puritans. This rings true. For us it was reflected in an austere attitude to life, a contempt for materialism, commitment to "the family," and the pervading sense that we were different, hewn from another quarry than the conformist crowds who could not think for themselves or stand on their own two feet and who went along with the latest trend. Concern for temperance, prison re-form, the abolition of capital punishment, active trade union member-ship, and other espousals of older, Quaker values were all there in the beginning in the family culture, only to yield in due course to more pessimistic and conservative opinions.

For me, church attendance was a rare occurrence. The church to which we did not go was the local Baptist church, the nearest equivalent to the religious family history I have described. We felt vaguely con-nected to it. As it was, the church represented the fading embers of a dying nonconformist culture. It was on the rocks, demographic changes having left it with a small and untutored, though sincere, membership. In the early years my contact with the church was restricted to occa-sional Sunday school attendance, social events, and coffee mornings. Two older sisters were more keenly involved, and it was to be the weddings of older brothers and sisters in the church that would make me more familiar with it. Like many, my adolescent years were accompanied by spiritual longings awakened in part by attendance, without any commitment, at a Billy Graham Crusade in 1960. Conversion came without particular drama, but as a definite shift, at the age of fifteen through attending the Catacombs Coffee Bar, an adventurous (for the times) new initiative in evangelism in the city center. Baptism and church membership were soon to follow, aided by the ministry of a new pastor.

In outward terms there was very little to inspire and encourage faith in the church situation. It rapidly became clear to me that whatever the Church was supposed to be, the church I was attending was not it. A seminal and yet hugely influential thought was conceived at that time, concerning the contrast between New Testament Christianity and the Church it actually was. Everything about the Church cried out to be transformed, and that basic perception has remained as the seed-bed for spiritual renewal. It is a small acorn from which middle-sized oaks have grown. But—and here the background made its impress—discovering the gospel felt like a discovery of identity, a becoming whole and fully human. It did not involve the crossing of huge cultural barriers as it does for some. To speak of "life" in Christ was a reality.

The mid-1960s were the years when charismatic renewal was making inroads into the mainstream Church. No sooner was I converted, therefore, than I came up against the charismatic movement. Initially this was through reading David Wilkerson's book *The Cross and the Switchblade*, which introduced the subject of baptism in the Spirit and speaking in tongues in the final chapter. I was both attracted by the vital spiritual life described and repelled (theologically ignorant though I was at this stage) by the theological language in which it was packaged—a state of affairs that has endured. Yet it was inevitable, given the climate of the times, that at some point the crunch of the charismatic movement would have to be faced.

That point came during university years. Prior to that, times of intense spiritual awareness were not at all unknown. But university (I was a student of modern languages) brought contact with a wider circle and more varied experience, especially a young woman who was to become my wife. I discovered the gift of tongues in a soundproof language laboratory in the basement of the modern languages building.

This seemed appropriate. On reflection, I see that this experience had more to do with assurance of salvation than with spiritual power. I am of the opinion that the experiences which are often called "baptism of the Spirit" might properly be understood within the context of the doctrine of assurance. They are heart-warming moments when the knowledge of salvation wells up within the heart. To know that I too was not excluded from God's grace, but made its object, did a lot for me, giving a spiritual impetus that was to lead to a vocation to the ministry on completing university.

Training for the ministry and studying theology added a great deal for which I am immensely grateful, but little that is directly relevant to the pilgrimage in renewal. There was a series of questions that few had yet learned to ask. Renewal was a personal experience (suspiciously regarded by many at that time), the implications of which were not immediately obvious for the corporate life of the Church, at least not to me. As an ordained minister from 1973, and in my first pastoral charge, the experience may have added something to the genuineness and sincerity of the ministry, but how the church itself was to be renewed was not yet at all clear. For five years I sought to learn my trade and to do the things that were expected. There was definite progress and return for the labor. The church grew steadily as a traditional but open and increasingly evangelical Baptist church. I had my first experiences of deliverance ministry, and this sharpened ideas of spiritual authority and conflict. People seemed to think well of me.

Unpopularity began to set in with the growth of the Restoration movement. This movement seemed to answer some of the hidden longings of the heart. Here was the language of the kingdom of God, which was familiar to me from my theological study, but expressed in a way that made it bankable because it was made to apply to ministry and to relationships. Most of all, here was the conviction that the Church itself needed to be renewed and restored, that the new wine of spiritual experience demanded also the new wineskins of reformed structures. I recognized in this that my early experience had by extension a community dimension to it which was to do with the worship of the Church and the common life of the people of God. This tied in with the innate sense I had had from the beginning, that the Church today was falling short of its true nature and intention. Reasonably successful though I had been as a minister to this point, I recognized that there were severe limits to my abilities, and the Restorationist teaching concerning a variety of ministries complementing each other appealed strongly. I could see the sense of fostering committed relationships with other leaders and churches, and the need for the "apostolic" dimension to provide the depths of wisdom and insight that were beyond me. As the church was changing and I was coming into the firing line, I also felt increasingly alone.

Attractive though Restorationism was, and eager though we were to attend the Dales Bible Week, I held reservations that led in due course to a parting of the ways. I had great unease concerning the emphasis on authority and submission, and came to reject strongly both the idea of delegated authority as taught in the movement and the justification of male dominance. It was at this point that I began to become a Baptist. This seems a strange thing for a Baptist minister to say, but I mean by it that I went beyond the outer form of Baptist theology to a greater understanding of its inner logic. I saw that it was to do with freedom, freedom for conscience and for the local church, and a vision of a free society.

These lines of thought were to lead in 1986, somewhat later than the time I am describing, to the publication of *The Radical Kingdom: Restoration in Theory and Practice*, a critique of Restorationism from the perspective of freedom. In 1980 Judy and I with our children spent a sabbatical period in Pennsylvania in a Mennonite community. A firm interest in the sixteenth-century continental movement known as Anabaptism had begun to take root, partly I suspect because of the Anabaptist, Hutterite echoes in my own family history. These groups of radical, revolutionary disciples caught my imagination, combining as they did a desire for the restoration of the true Church with zeal to the point of martyrdom. Here was a historical vantage point, itself pointing back to the New Testament, which provided a lens through which to view the contemporary Church in both its traditional and its innovative modes of life. I saw that persistently throughout history movements had arisen with the same radical desire to be true to the New Testament vision of the Church, and many of them had left a clear mark on social history and development that seemed to indicate a link between the renewal of the Church and the transformation and progress of culture.

All of this gave a sense of confidence in developing an independent perspective on the needs of the modern Church.

Meanwhile, back at the church, we were beginning to experiment. I had managed to persuade people, just about, that the Restorationist pathway was not for us. As an alternative I offered a vision of being true to our own heritage of freedom, but at the same time incorporating into it what we perceived to be the strengths of Restorationism. We established an eldership and developed friendships with Christian leaders who could exercise an apostolic function toward us. All of this worked tolerably well. I myself began to meet with a cluster of other pastors, and we found strength and encouragement in this. The church grew numerically, changed progressively into a new order of church life, and evolved a distinctive new self-understanding.

It was this church, already embracing charismatic renewal, that experienced, in June 1982, a visit from John Wimber and his team. I had heard rumors that David Watson had invited for a visit some people from Yorba Linda, wherever that was, and that unusual things had happened. Friends in the Bible Society suggested to us and to others that we might like to invite these same people to our churches to give them an opportunity to minister in Free Churches. As they were paying for themselves, this seemed like a good idea. We were not really expecting what happened.

The visit was billed as a Renewal Weekend on the subject of power evangelism. The visitors from California, fragrant and gum-chewing, were an instant hit. John Wimber had worked hard on producing a worthy argument on the benefits of power evangelism. The first part of the weekend was dedicated to his exposition of this subject, which, it must be said, did not go down too well. It was not the content which made it dull but the manner of its delivery. John stumbled through a detailed paper, often tripping over his own words. I began to wonder whether I had made the right decision. The people, whom I had urged to attend on pain of death, were restless. I say all of this to indicate that there was no expectation of what was to happen next, and certainly no suggestion of how we were to behave.

On the Saturday afternoon John announced that he had talked enough and that it was time to have some fun. He introduced an aging hippy named Lonnie Frisbee. Lonnie led us in the singing of a short song, and then, having climbed into the pulpit, uttered the words: "Come, Holy Spirit." What happened next is exceedingly difficult to describe. Within seconds the Spirit of God had fallen upon a large proportion of the congregation, many of whom were trembling and shaking, speaking in tongues, calling on the Lord, prophesying, and some of whom (hard though it might seem to believe) were flapping up and down like fish upon the floor. Some of this I was able to see, but most of it passed me by since I was doing the same. The gum-chewing visitors were now coming into their own, "blessing" those who were responding and exhorting the Lord to "Give him/her more!" It was all quite astonishing, but, it has to be said, hugely enjoyable. For myself, a split-second decision had to be made as to whether this was of God. I decided it was. This was a decision made upon instinct, as time to apply the usual tests (does it produce fruit, etc.) was in short supply. Even in the midst of it there was a calm and a personal detachment which meant that what was happening was not against my will.

The weekend, and indeed the whole week in different congregations, continued in the same manner. It was our first experience of spiritual power in this way, and it opened our eyes to the meaning of Pentecost. We could understand why the first Christians could be accused of drunkenness. We began to take with a new seriousness the dramatic encounters with God that are recorded in Scripture and the strange phenomena which would sometimes accompany them. The months following this event were times of intense spiritual ministry, much of it in the area of inner healing and deliverance. There was a sense of people being purged and prepared. A great deal was learned in this period, and it felt as if we were on the boundaries of the spiritual life.

The visit of John Wimber, among other things, strengthened us in our sense of self-confidence. Having opted not to become Restorationists, the visit confirmed us in this step. In the developing movement around John we saw a set of values quite differently articulated from those of Restorationism. Whereas the latter movement tended toward sectarianism, building barriers between itself and the rest of the Church, John Wimber was keen to break those barriers down, to affirm God's love for the Church in all its forms of existence. His model of the Church was one which was open and welcoming—in his own language, a "bounded center" focusing on Christ at the center rather than a "bounded set" focusing on who belonged and who did not. All these insights were added thankfully to the distinctive concoction we were in the process of brewing. It goes without saying that in its development the church had not been successful in persuading everybody to make the continuing journey. Some had opted to join other churches. In retrospect, it was amazing how calmly the church responded to and absorbed the Wimber visit. Subsequent years saw further visits to the church, not from John Wimber himself, although his visits to the country kept us in touch, but from associates, each of whom brought something distinctive and worthwhile. This was a golden period of spiritual growth and learning, and also a time when we sought to impart to others what had been given to us.

It must also be said that this whole experience brought its problems. There is a short step between knowing what it is to tremble when the Spirit comes and thinking that if we tremble the Spirit is bound to come. It is also the case that spiritual phenomena are a mixed blessing, as was argued in rigorous detail by Jonathan Edwards in the eighteenth century. In the wake of Wimber we learned to distinguish between healthy phenomena and unhealthy, and that even the healthy can degenerate to the point that they are of neither use nor ornament. We learned there was a time to stop shaking. All of this I see as the process of pruning a healthy tree in order that it may grow all the better. We also encountered the phenomenon of burnout, that intense spiritual experiences can give way, perhaps must give way, to a barrenness of spirit. After mountaintop experiences, where is there to go but back down into the valley? And perhaps this must be so, since God is always greater than the experiences we have of Him and therefore our experiences need to drop away so that we are dealing with God himself.

And so the pilgrimage moves on. For me the challenge became to channel the spiritual energy we had been given into growth. The years that followed the visitation of the Spirit were years marked by conversions, church growth, and church planting. All of this is easy to say, but at the time it was exhausting, costly, and time-consuming. In the midst of all this activity a profound urge was reawakened within me. It was to do with theology.

It appears to me that a feature of the aftermath of renewal is a deep hunger for understanding, and that this is a mark of its authenticity. The criticism that charismatic renewal is more concerned with romanticism than enlightenment has been only partly true. Charismatic renewal has been concerned to redress a balance, the over-intellectualizing of the faith and the neglect of the heart and the emotions. It has led to a greater wholeness or completeness. It has been concerned to rediscover the intuitive dimensions of the human soul, to complement the analytical. All of this was not before time. Yet now this very concern to rediscover the heart is being accompanied by a new concern for learning. Conferences which offer the opportunity for reflection are being widely appreciated. Many are giving themselves to deeper study. In short, there is a new concern for theology, the study of God.

I felt God calling me to be a theological teacher, at least for a time. I see this as different from a teacher of theology. The first is an office in the church, the second in an institution. Of course, both offices might just coincide, but the important insight is that good theology is a service to the Church. It is not dictating what may or may not be believed but reflecting on what the Church does believe in the light of her Scriptures, her tradition, and her mission to the contemporary world. It became clear to me that wherever there is abundant spiritual energy allied to a less than adequate theology, trouble will ensue. It having seemed at one point crucial to mobilize the church and see it renewed (a task only just begun, I admit), once life was in evidence it became equally important that it move in the right direction. I had observed, for instance, how the heady ministry of deliverance could go astray with relative ease, and how the safeguards against this must ultimately concern the way we think about evil—in other words they are theological. These reflections found expression in a book, *The Fair Face of Evil: Putting the Power of Darkness in its Place*, published in 1988. Renewal needed to be reflected upon in order to be preserved.

In 1986 I resigned my pastorate after thirteen years and spent a year in theological research, primarily concerned with the theology of Karl Barth. Since 1987 I have been teaching Christian Doctrine and helping to train ministers in one of the Baptist theological colleges. Having had time to think further, I sometimes ask myself what is now important to me in the continuing pilgrimage. Perhaps I can attempt some of these tentative thoughts at this point.

It is important to affirm and not disown that which has been gained so far. I say this because life is always an experience of broadening and extension, and in this process it is possible to look back deprecatingly upon past experiences and even to react against them. This does not appear to me to be a profitable means of progress. The typical divergent thinker inevitably becomes dissatisfied and possibly also tired with categories and experiences that serve their purpose and then begin to look incomplete. This is a healthy process, otherwise we are led to an idolatry of the past when what is important is the living God in the present and in the future. Yet we are each the subject of our own history and do ourselves no good when we disown this fact. Progress into the future comes from owning the good things that belong to the past and yet seeing them within ever new and ever fuller contexts. In that sense I wish to affirm those things that have been of help in the past. Char-ismatic renewal has brought untold blessing to the Church, and the face of the Church in this country is markedly different, and positively so, from when I first encountered it.

At the same time, it does appear to me that charismatic renewal is merging again with the primary traditions of the Church's life and becoming less an entity in itself and more a seasoning and a dimension in the totality of the Church's life. In more theological terms, having emphasized the Spirit and sought to give Him place, there is now an entirely consistent and appropriate need to become fully trinitarian. It is here that the health of the whole Church lies, and a most encouraging sign in modern theology is the place given not only to the doctrine of the Trinity but to the trinitarian shape of Christian existence and of all truly Christian thought. Ultimately our concern is with God, and how we conceive Him shapes our attitude to all other realities. To maintain its health and develop its impetus the movement must avoid unitarian-isms of the Spirit and the Son and explore the depths of the Church's trinitarian heritage.

Having spent much of my life concerned for the renewal of the Church, it has become increasingly clear to me that the renewing of the Church and the transformation of God's world are parallel and related themes. If the renewal of the Church is a priority, it is so because the Church has a mission to fulfil and is involved with God in His work of redemption and transformation. A further stage of my own pilgrimage has been defined by this imperative, wishing to see the saving work of Christ as the expression of the love of God for the whole of His creation. Insofar as charismatic renewal fails to gain this perspective, it will prove to be a capitulation of our culture's desire to privatize religious experience and so domesticate it. This tendency is already clear in some parts of the world where charismatic experience and reactionary politics have become closely allied. I am convinced that this pitfall can only be avoided through a more adequate ecclesiology, seeing the Church as the avant-garde of God's future kingdom, called to realize in the present a form of life that has prophetic quality and which may therefore act transformingly upon the wider culture. With the proper theological perspectives, the renewing of the Church and radical influence within our culture could become mutually beneficial partners, with the first providing the sustaining spirituality for the second, and the second the necessary expression for the first. It is in this realm that personal and corporate challenges for the renewal movement are pressing upon us.

Some time ago I came across the idea of the "second naiveté," and it spoke powerfully to me. The idea was being used in the context of studying the Bible. When first we come to faith, the Bible lives for us and speaks to us and we take it pretty much as it is. But then we learn to analyze and to dissect, especially if we study theology. We run the risk of failing to see the wood for the trees and of not hearing the word of the Lord. But beyond critical analysis there is a further place to be reached, that of coming humbly again to the Holy Scriptures with the expectation that we will be addressed there by the living God. This is the place of the second naiveté, and it is a good place, for this time we approach God's Word with all that we have gained from our critical study and we are likely to hear the Word of God at new depths and with greater force.

After the period of enthusiasm the charismatic movement has yielded to the period of reflection. This is where we now are, and this book is part of the process. The reflection is a necessary part of discerning that which is good in order that we may hold fast to it. It is clear enough that there are spurious phenomena, superficial judgements, manufactured experiences, manipulative actions, as indeed there are in all the varieties of religious experience. To see these for what they are is good. But beyond the place of critical examination there is the place of second naiveté, where we acknowledge that we need God and need His Spirit. And this place is a wiser place precisely because we have seen the pitfalls and have grown in wisdom. All the basic charismatic affirmations about our need for the Holy Spirit and His gifts are as valid now as they ever were. The enduring value of the charismatic movement is that it points us beyond itself to the one who is the Lord and Giver of life, of whom we shall always stand in constant need.

TEN

Notes From a Wayward Son

ANDREW WALKER

As every boy from Eton knows: there is only one other school (even through Harrow has recently dropped like a stone down the tables of the top educational establishments). This sense of identifying oneself over and against the significant "other" is familiar to me, for I was born in the Elim Foursquare Gospel Church, and for us there was no other church of equal standing save our great rival-cousin—Assemblies of God.

It was not that we did not know of any other churches. We knew of the Christian Brethren (smart but suspect) and the Baptists and Methodists (dead as dodos). Because I was brought up in Tonypandy and Neath in Glamorgan, Wales, until I was eight, I knew of Ebenezer Chapel as something quintessentially yet mysteriously Welsh. Of more significance was acquaintance with the Apostolic Church, a small Pentecostal denomination with nearby headquarters which, we were told, sported doubtful credentials.

As for Anglicans, we knew that they were religious but we doubted if they could be "saved" because they believed in infant baptism and did not seem to understand, so we thought, the need for conversion. But even I knew they were better than Catholics, who were apostates and sinners. Certain members of our congregation whispered that nuns killed babies and that the pope was the "whore of Babylon" (though I never did understand this exotic reference).

Years later, when I was in London in the early 1960s, I used to hear similar things said at Hyde Park Corner in the name of Protestant truth, and less rabid but equally condemning things from a certain separatist Calvinist chapel at Westminster.

Except for the Assemblies of God, where I knew of (but nothing about) Donald Gee and Nelson J. Parr, my life was surrounded by the great names of our church: Pastors W. G. Hathaway, W. Greenwood, P. Brewster, and what was already then a living but tarnished legend, Principal George Jeffreys. To be frank, we never talked of Jeffreys in the present tense: he was that great evangelist of the past.

It might be thought that it must have been strange living in such a small denomination so out of concert with the mainstream churches and so out of touch with the world. In fact, it was not strange at all. Son, as I was, of an Elim pastor, and with a mother who was also a preacher and singer, the Elim movement was the main focus of my life. It may have been small, but it did not seem so to me, for we were always mixing with other Elim members in special meetings and conventions.

Life was circumscribed by the church and my parents' commitments. I went to Elim three times on Sunday, often on Saturday, sometimes to the mid-week prayer meeting. Our entertainment was the church, which doubled as chapel and music hall. There was great talent within Elim (there probably still is), and we enjoyed and expected a good sing and dramatic presentations of the gospel. Long before it became normative in mainstream churches, we were playing guitars, singing in quartets, shaking tambourines, and sometimes clapping our hands and tapping our feet (though this was going too far for some pastors).

It meant, therefore, that although the world was officially banished from our doors—there was no drinking, smoking, going to the theatre, cinema, or dance hall—we would sway to our beloved choruses set to waltz, march, swing, or sanitized ragtime.

Our response to the arts was sectarian. Not only did we officially eschew popular music, there was also little interest in either classical or modern composers. Indeed, there was little investment in high cul-ture. Good reading, for example, was not so much forbidden as ignored. Other children may have read *A Tale of Two Cities* and *Tess of the D'Urbervilles*, but I read *Edgar Nelthorpe* and *Eric: Or Little by Little*. Enid

Blyton's books were encouraged when we were younger, along with Christian novels such as *Treasures of the Snow*, but there was no partic-ular encouragement to read the standard children's classics such as *The Wind in the Willows* or *Winnie the Pooh*. When I went to grammar school at the age of seventeen, all my middle-class Christian friends were weaned on C. S. Lewis's *The Lion, the Witch, and the Wardrobe*. I'd never heard of it.

We may never have gone to the plays of Noel Coward or Shake-speare, but we were not short of drama. The Holy Spirit moved among us with power, so we fervently believed, though our meetings were usually very jolly and unassuming. There would be prophecies and tongues, healings, and testimonies of wondrous happenings. At times the jolliness would become sheer excitement and it would seem as if the building would rock with the thrill of it all. And yet to me, as a small boy, it was just what we did in our church, and was no more bizarre than I imagine reciting the Office together would be for the staunch Anglican.

Sometimes we held "Great Divine Healing Crusades," though this was more a declaration of hope than a description of reality. God was with us and we felt Him in our midst and heard Him through prophecies and the interpretations of strange tongues (though for the life of me I cannot remember a single prophecy from those times).

We would swoon at the latest adventist teachings, which always seemed to predict that we were poised on the edge of disaster, the world about to be plunged into Armageddon, while we were whisked away to meet Jesus in the clouds.

This had a great effect on me as a small child. I remember one day getting out of bed and going into my parents' room, only to find them absent. They did not respond to my call, and I was suddenly overcome with dread at the thought that "the rapture" had taken place and I had been left behind.

The biblical prophecies also fueled my starved intellect. Fundamen-talists as we were, prophetic interpretations were a legitimate source of imaginative, albeit fantastical, speculations. *The Mark of the Beast* was one particularly lurid book about the Antichrist I remember reading and enjoying. I liked stories about demons, too (exorcisms were, in fact, part of the repertoire of Pentecostalism but we rarely practiced them).

I was not considered to be a particularly bright child. School was a strain for me: it reinforced my belief in the wickedness of the world and the perfidiousness of lost souls. It was not a place to learn from; it was more a place in which to show off. I was not particularly popular with other children, partly because I was different, being Elim, but mainly because I was a "big-head." It was amazing, for one who knew so little about the world, how much I had to say about it.

Showing off was of course frowned upon in Elim unless it was done in the interests of the church. So if you could sing a bit, which I could, and talk the proverbial hind leg off the donkey, then showing off was allowed under the guise of singing sacred solos, giving testimonies, or preaching. But at school I liked to show off through acting in plays. It was the only time I remember being praised by the teachers.

Predictably, at the age of eleven I failed to gain a place at a grammar school, but my primary leaver's report promised that my acting ability would get me far; there was no mention of my brains. In fact, going to secondary school opened up the first fissure in my world view. We had two teachers, "Basher Brooks" and "Toby Twirl," who thought that I was not a complete dunce. They introduced me to literature and a love of history, and helped me to move on to the grammar school when I was seventeen, in 1962.

But the crucial spiritual period of my young life was 1959–60. My father had been ill for a long time, having suffered a stroke in 1957. It changed his personality, and it was difficult for him to cope with my precocious presence. And then, when I was away at a camp in August 1959, with young people from churches other than Elim, my father died unexpectedly. I was not taken to his funeral, and my anger at this, and my guilt for upsetting him in his final years, lived with me well into adulthood.

There was no pension from the church and nowhere to live when my father died, so my mother rented a small bungalow from a Strict Baptist. (This may seem a curious fact to remember, but the denominational tag was for us, in those days, a primary means of personal identification.) We had very little money, but living in our new home was a time of great comfort to my mother and me, for not only were we close, there was also a great deal of religious activity to keep us occupied (my sister kept her counsel about father's death, and soon moved on to university).

I was nominally Christian from the age of twelve, and intellectually a convinced Elimite, but religion did not really fire me in any way. By now I was a teenager, with an interest in bikes and cricket, the cinema—which I used to sneak into without telling mother—and girls.

It was April 1960, when I was still fourteen years of age, that I finally found out for myself what Pentecost was all about. I was visiting Neath in South Wales, where I used to live as a small boy. On the Easter Monday I was sick and could not go hear the flown-in American speaker at the Elim "city temple." Later in the day I recovered, and although I knew they were supposed to be suspect, I wandered down to the local Apostolic church, which was holding its own convention.

Much of the service was in Welsh, but I remember it as cracking with energy and rippling with congregational excitement. I noticed a girl who was showing an inch of petticoat below her knee. (She noticed me noticing her, and pulled her skirt a little higher.) During one of the intervals I approached her and tried what I hoped was casual but sophisticated chat (so necessary to me in those days, for I was barely five feet tall!). Her brother—who was on crutches, I remember—cornered me outside and threatened to do me harm if I tried any "funny stuff"! And then we went back inside.

It was now evening. The pastor invited all those who wanted to "tarry for the Spirit" to come to the front. I went, though I have no idea whether it was true longing for God or bravado—or both. The pretty young girl came out, too, but she was some distance away from me. We knelt in a prayer line against the mahogany nonconformist pew. I prayed for the Spirit with fervor but little expectation. One of our church members, some time previously, had told of waiting on the Spirit for nigh on twenty years, so I was not assuming that the "baptism" was an automatic right.

I was at the end of the line. When the pastor reached me he put his hands on my head. Something happened which was unexpectedly physical. I felt from his hands what these days a New Ager might call "waves of energy," and then my tongue locked solid, and the Walker of the chat was struck dumb. I tried to talk, but all I could manage was a stammer of disconnected sounds. Then the sounds connected and the tongues rushed out, and I felt good but strange, and a little frightened.

So this was the baptism! I set off for home, which was no less than the manse of the Elim church. I staggered about the street like a drunk. This is what I thought at the time, not knowing firsthand the perils of alcohol. (Looking back, and with a more varied experience than I had then, I think "feeling drunk" was an excellent analogy.) The pastor at the manse, whose name I have forgotten, poured cold water on my baptism of fire (it was, remember, from the hands of the less than favored Apostolics), and I went to bed dispirited, only to wake up in the night, merrily pealing away with a fresh triple of the tongues.

It has to be said, as a matter of fact, whatever spiritual or psychological interpretation we might want to put on it, the "baptism in the Holy Spirit" changed me radically. Where before I had been indifferent to Pentecost, now I was fervent about it. Zeal, rather than goodness, would probably be a fair description of me at that time, for I soon found that Pentecostal experience did not of itself bring the long-suffering fruits of the Spirit.

On the contrary. For although I now became an evangelist and boy-preacher, I also became more conceited than I had been before the "baptism"—if such a thing were possible!—and my increased swagger and cockiness meant that I made enemies at school. At church I became a gospel singer who played guitar; delusions of grandeur in this area were to accompany me long after I abandoned Pentecostalism. More significantly, I also became a soul-winner in the best Elim tradition. No boy was safe from me at school. I remember the time I confronted twins at the urinals, where I insisted they could not leave until they made a decision for Christ. One was saved and the other got away!

Soon I had organized a Christian Union. Several boys were converted (one still attends the Elim church in Worthing) and we had lively if idiosyncratic Bible studies. I became head boy, and after a shaky start, went on to grammar school. By now I was running an evangelistic youth team and was as committed a Pentecostal as I have ever been, but after 1961 I ceased to be a member of Elim.

It is difficult to say why this happened. I drifted away rather than choosing to leave on a point of principle. My reference group had changed. When I got to the grammar school my friends were mainly middle-class, and if they had any religious allegiance it was to the Church of England. I began to attend an Anglican evangelical church, but I never joined (or was invited to, for that matter). There were more and "posher" girls there, and one stunning girl, who attended the Sunday night "Squash," led me effortlessly away from the inner sanctum of evangelical piety.

She was glamorous and worldly-wise, smoked Gitanes, and was rich. More intoxicated with the girl than with God, I went to London Bible College in 1964—not wanting to do so, but feeling that I ought to for the sake of my mother, because I had promised her that I would go.

I must have been the College's most inglorious son, for I only stayed a term, feigning a mental breakdown in order to get out. Quite suddenly I stopped believing in God. No doubt this had nothing to do with London Bible College, but when I left I dropped Pentecostalism—and all things religious—for, so I thought, wider shores.

By now my soul and senses were full of the sounds and enticements of the Sixties. For seven years I did without God and made do with sociology, pop music, and armchair socialism. I never took the Marxist bait, partly because I was not persuaded intellectually by its Hegelian dialectic, but mainly because the Marxists I met reminded me too much, in terms of psychological profile, of the Pentecostals I had left behind. I was still interested in religion from a sociological standpoint, but eschewed emotionalism and what I had come to believe was psychic mumbo-jumbo.

In fact, that is putting it in too cerebral a fashion. I had become allergic to all things evangelical and Pentecostal. If I had been asked to write of Elim at that time, I would have come up with something of the bile and squinted version of Jeanette Winterson's *Oranges Are Not the Only Fruit.* I was not so much ashamed of my background as contemptuous of it: like Ms. Winterson, I liked to think of myself as the butterfly who had escaped from the claustrophobic chrysalis.

And then in 1971—after the usual twists and turns of coping with adult life in the present age—I found God again as suddenly as I had lost Him. Or to be exact, He found me—and in a way that was both typically Pentecostal and yet atypical: it happened in a dream.

I was on a modern dance floor, and I was a teenager again. The room was noisy and crowded, but then directly in front of me a man from the crowd came into focus, and it was Jesus. He asked me to dance. I protested, for we Pentecostals did not dance. The invitation not only took me by surprise, it also embarrassed me: how could I dance with *Him*? How could He ask *me* to do such a thing?

And then the Lord spoke to me (I say the Lord advisedly, for the Jesus of this dream was not a figure that in any way resembled a familiar friend). He said, "If you do not dance with me, I can have no part of you." I knew I had to do it or He would turn away, so I lifted my right hand to take His left and I extended my left arm to embrace His right, and like a young girl I was led away on a merry dance that had something of the character of a quickstep or a Gay Gordon. I was desperately happy.

Of course such intense emotion recollected in waking tranquility would lead, one might imagine, to an instant debunking: a cold dose of psychological reductionism. And indeed there were no doubt many personal circumstances at the time that could be said to have brought on the dream. But the fact is that when I awoke I was a believer in a Christian God again, and it never occurred to me to interpret the story in terms of, say, repressed homo-eroticism, or spicy food, let alone unhappy circumstances.

Since that day in 1971 I have, from time to time, examined the dream-encounter in more or less objective fashion, but although the vividness of the dance has faded, my belief in the Lord of that dance has not. I also learned another lesson from the dream that has stayed with me ever since: experience does not always come with a ready-made theology. To believe in a God again, as I did then, was one thing, but how was I to understand Him? I was surprised to find that I did not want to go back to the church of my youth. This discovery was reinforced by my rediscovering the Bible. Or rather my discovery of it: for it was so long since I had read it with evangelical eyes that the much-loved scriptural passages of my childhood seemed strange and enigmatic.

This led to a determination to begin from scratch, and for me that meant beginning with church history. It came as a bit of a shock to discover that there were fifteen hundred years of vibrant and exciting Christian witness before the Reformation. As a boy I had swallowed the usual sectarian interpretation of Christianity: that there was Jesus, the Bible, and me—church history was not high on the list of Pentecostal priorities. But in reading the history I became excited at the development of Christian doctrine down the ages. I remember in particular reading for the first time J.N.D. Kelly's *Early Christian Doctrines* and being stunned by the brilliance of the early church Fathers (and to think I had wasted all these years studying sociology!).

Indeed, so immersed did I become in the history of the early church that I changed the direction of my post-graduate studies so that I could relate the theology of the Fathers to the issues of present-day social science. I recall that my supervisor received a curt note from the London University board of sociological studies enquiring whether my doctorate, "Two Versions of Sociological Discourse: The Apophatic and Cataphatic Grounds of Social Science," was on the level!

It was also in 1971 that I encountered for the first time the charismatic renewal movement. I soon discovered that a charismatic was a middle-class Pentecostal (a conviction that remains with me still). It was strange for me, as an ex-Elimite, to find the Pentecostal experience at large in the mainstream churches. I sought out some Catholic charismatics who were my neighbors in southwest London. They were graciously accepting of me—caught as I was in a denominational no-man's-land—and their friendship did much to lessen my prejudice against Roman Catholics. I was more amused than bemused to find them speaking in tongues and praying over each other, yet without any of the pious trappings of my childhood. They drank alcohol and smoked (and sometimes even swore) and refused to take themselves too seriously.

And yet, for them, Pentecost was a serious business: it had lifted them out of nominal Catholicism into a committed Christianity. "The baptism" had something of a conversion experience about it: there was nothing more important to them than their newfound faith. Their Pentecost was anarchic and liberating, breaking them free from the boundaries of ritual and dogma. And yet, among some of the them, it had also led to a fey spirituality: morality ran wild, and a number of people were seriously hurt and bewildered as they discovered, as I had as a young boy, that Pentecostal experience does not automatically lead to holiness, sound judgment, or moral sensibility.

Not that I was any less of a mess than they were—far from it—but for the first time since my days as a Pentecostal I began to sense some worth in my upbringing. We were narrow, but there was depth. Certainly we were puritanical, but there was something of the high Puritan idealism among us. There was not much scholarship in evidence, but we were not stupid. (How I have longed, as a professional watcher of the charismatic "stars" over the years, that some of the modern-day charismatics had an ounce of that working-class "nous" of the Pentecostals who could more often than not sniff out a "wrong-un" or spot the latest supernatural fashion as no more than a passing wind.)

Despite the mixed blessings of the Roman Catholic renewal, I already knew in 1971 that I was beginning to turn toward Catholicism, or at least sacramentalism. But I found Roman Catholic liturgy alien to me and I felt that the papal claims were unconvincing in the light of my studies of early church history. I had already read Timothy Ware's *The Orthodox Church*, and was fascinated to have stumbled across a tradition that was curiously both mystical and yet down-to-earth. And then one night on television I saw Archbishop Anthony Bloom, as he was then, in conversation with Marghanita Laski.

I was deeply impressed by his graciousness and intellectual toughness, so I rang the Russian Orthodox Church and requested an interview, ostensibly to talk about the Russian revolution. It was disconcerting to have this perfectly relaxed archbishop smiling in agreement with me while I fidgeted away in a denunciation of the Orthodox Church and all its reactionary ways. (I was a sociologist, and a socialist of a kind, and thought this was one way to put him on the defensive.) When I paused for breath, and because I did not really have anything else to say, there was a long silence, the archbishop looked straight at me. After what seemed an unnaturally long wait, he said, "Now tell me, why have you really come to see me?"

And so it began—the journey to Orthodoxy which was to lead to my joining the Russian Church in 1973. The sheer sensuality of the Russian liturgy was at first an offense to my Pentecostal puritanism. I used to stand in the church with my eyes closed so that I would not have to see all the colors, icons, and the unregimented bobbings and crossings of the faithful at prayer. The music would overwhelm me with its richness and solemn emotion, and in the darkness, despite the pungent incense, it was almost like being back in the Welsh valleys with the male-voice choirs and the *hwyl* of the Apostolic Church.

Of course in time I adjusted, and became a Pentecostal exile in a diaspora church whose own experience has been "singing the Lord's song in a strange land." I discovered that Orthodoxy had its own charismatic tradition, but that its cultural and spiritual roots lay in Eastern spirituality and contemplative prayer rather than in Western enthusiasm and frenetic singing. To this day, I believe that the sobriety of silence in the Eastern Church is one of the lost chords in the charismatic melody.

Perhaps more significantly, I learned from Orthodoxy that God the Holy Spirit is a person not a power, and that this same person who brooded over the waters of creation also overshadowed the maiden of Israel, raised Jesus from the dead, and continues to bring to the Church all that God the Father has revealed through the Son. The Spirit can therefore never be raw power without sacrificial love, intuitive and psychic force without sober counsel, a strong advocate on our behalf without also convicting us of wrongdoing.

But Russian Orthodoxy was to do something else for me in terms of my Pentecostal past and my continuing involvement with the renewal in the present. Orthodoxy stresses the healing-and-restoration model of forgiveness perhaps more than the juridical one. To be forgiven also leads to reconciliation. For me, this reconciliation started when Metropolitan Anthony (as the archbishop had now become) was able to show me that I was not coming to the Orthodox Church to find Christ: I had already discovered Him as a young man, and now He was leading me to the Church.

Furthermore, he insisted, for me to become Orthodox would be counterproductive if I thought that I could exchange one religious ghetto for the enclosedness of another. Because of my past, he told me, I should try to build bridges between the Orthodox tradition and the other Christian confessions who were out of communion, or not of sympathy, with the Eastern Church (or more to the point, as I discovered, just plain ignorant of it).

This pastoral advice was, in fact, to become the latent spring of the C. S. Lewis Centre, which was founded in 1987; but in the 1970s the immediate effect was for me to begin to shed my shame and bitterness for my sectarian past and to reappraise it without rancor.

I learned to appreciate—as did the Anglican C. F. Andrews, when looking back on his childhood in the Catholic Apostolic Church—that the Spirit is sovereign: He blows where He wills, and breathes life into the most unlikely and least promising of organisms.

Elim means "place of refreshing" in Hebrew, and if it also had its stagnant pools it was not without its vigorous spas. For it was in Elim that I first learned that

Jesus loves the little children,
all the children in the world.
Red and yellow, black and white,
all are precious in his sight.
Jesus loves the little children of the world.

There was incipient racism there, as in all churches, but I never doubted that humanity was by definition a co-humanity under one God.

It was in Elim that I first learned of the centrality of repentance in the Christian life: "At the cross, at the cross where I first saw the light and the burden of my heart rolled away." It was in Orthodoxy that I was to find the fulfillment of that message, for I discovered that being "down at the cross" was not a psychological expurgation of guilt but a continuous process of self-losing and spiritual renewal.

What we might call the ceaseless need for repentance is endemic in Orthodox spirituality. "Lord Jesus Christ, Son of God, have mercy on me, a sinner" runs the Jesus Prayer: there lies the antidote to charismatic triumphalism and the messianic pretension that bedevils Pentecostal movements.

But being reconciled with the Elim of my past was to bring to mind a rude good health that, notwithstanding a certain crankiness, never entirely gave way to the mountebanks and mavericks of the charismatic fringes. There is a lesson here for the Renewal. Elim and the Assemblies of God have a long tradition of making mistakes: they have been going about their Pentecostal business for eighty years and have learned from their errors and misdemeanors.

The charismatic renewal, being middle-class and new to the game, thinks it does not have much to learn from its older and less fashionable cousin. It is mistaken. Classical Pentecostals may still be Bible fundamentalists, yet at least they have fallen into the habit of "testing all things" not by the vagaries and uncertainties of so-called spiritual discernment, but by Scripture. Indeed their holiness tradition shines through, for they have not entirely lost Wesley's commitment to the quadrilaterals: faith, reason, Scripture, and experience. It is only when the experiential swamps Pentecostalism (whether classical or modern-day charismatic) that everything becomes unbalanced and those negative aspects of the tradition—sentimentality, fanaticism, the lust for power—come roaring through with the undiscriminating force of a tidal wave. What kind of religious revival will we see if these powers are loosed on the world?

Elim and the Assemblies of God have it within their resources to sound a restraining and correcting note to the present charismatic movement if they have the will to do so. It is hard to raise a voice, however, when you are made to feel second-class cousins, as classical Pentecostals so often are by both the historical denominations and the so-called "new churches." I remember that as a boy I could withstand opposition but not belittlement. Few people can stand up and be true to themselves when they are being looked down upon; so often the result of being either shunned or patronized by fellow Christians is to embrace the less uncomfortable ally of exlusivism and to rattle blunted sabres behind the buckler of inverted snobbery.

Today, however, Elim and the Assemblies of God have gained in confidence: they now have available nearly four generations of experience to draw on. Would that the renewal movement, and the house churches, had harkened to the wise warnings of pastor John Lancaster, when in an article in *Decision* magazine some years ago he wrote eirenically but incisively of "the cult of the self-conscious." I showed it to another wayward Pentecostalist, Professor Walter Hollenweger. He agreed with me that it was one of the most balanced and timely views of the charismatic movement he had seen, for this Elim pastor had put his finger on the dangers of leaders who had ceased to be God-centered and had become so self-conscious of their significance in the divine mission that they were not so much promoters of Pentecost as purveyors of their own (often profitable) wares.

I also showed the article to Metropolitan Anthony. "This is good," he said; "this is Orthodox." He meant, of course, that the criticisms of Pastor Lancaster were the sort of criticisms that would naturally flow from the Orthodox tradition: for Pentecostalism and Orthodoxy share a common view on the supernatural. They both fervently believe in miracles, and because of the seriousness with which they hold to that belief they both also insist that fraudulence, superstition, and shoddy spirituality should be exposed as an affront to the gospel. (At their worst, both Pentecostalism and Orthodoxy have a long history of "wonder-working" oddities, if not outright chicanery.)

Arthur Wallis, the late senior statesman of Restorationism, once referred to me, objectively enough, as an "ex-Pentecostal." Denominationally this is of course true. I have never, however, reneged on my past experience, even though I would have to say unequivocally that my churchmanship, theology, and spirituality are Orthodox. Since I became Orthodox, I have not been ashamed of being a former Pentecostal—nor, on the whole, do Pentecostals seem to be ashamed of me. Indeed it is surely one of the oddities of being an accredited lay preacher in the Orthodox Church that I have preached far more in charismatic churches than in Orthodox ones. Even stranger was my experience in 1988 when I was taken by an Orthodox priest in Tulsa, Oklahoma, to be introduced to the faculty of theology at Oral Roberts University. Later in the week I was to run a series of workshops at the St. Anne's Orthodox Institute attended by professors from Oral Roberts University! These encounters, which many might see as eccentric, are by no means atypical of my experience in North America and Europe over the last few years.

I well remember when I attended the World Council of Churches consultation on the Renewal in Switzerland in 1980. Naturally, I spent most of my time with the Orthodox delegation. They were curious about rather than censorious toward the charismatic crowd. ("Why do they jump around like Chinese crackers?" asked one of the priests from Lebanon.) However, the senior member of the party, Metropolitan Irenaeus from Crete, was particularly taken with a West Indian gospel group from a Pentecostal church in London. He bought one of their music tapes, and as he was stuffing it deep into his cassock I asked him if he had enjoyed their music. "No," he said, "I did not much like their songs, for they were too sentimental, but I was deeply impressed with the singers, and I want always to remember them. I feel that they are really like us inside."

Inside my heart Pentecostalism and Orthodoxy abide like the subject and interpreter of an unfinished biography: they are not interlinked like some mysterious monophysite conjunction; they are separated by time and experience, by preference and commitment, by intellectual conviction and, yes, by estrangement. But they have both had to come to terms with the fact that there is only one Spirit of truth, one Comforter, and in Him they have learned to exchange not merely a greeting, but a kiss.

Notes

Chapter 1

1. Yves Congar, *I Believe in the Holy Spirit* (London: Geoffrey Chapman, 1983).
2. The Doctrine Commission of the General Synod of the Church of England, *We Believe in the Holy Spirit* (London: Church House Publishing, 1991).
3. Ibid., p. 95.

Chapter 2

1. A basic introduction to the story of John Wimber, his impact upon the British scene and his teaching is that of John Gunstone, *Signs and Wonders: The Wimber Phenomenon* (London: Daybreak, 1989).
2. Some of the material in this section is drawn from a lecture by Professor G. R. Beasley-Murray, "An evaluation of John Wimber's interpretation of Scripture in reference to power healing and power evangelism," delivered at Spurgeon's College, September 14, 1988.
3. John Wimber with Kevin Springer, *Power Evangelism: Signs and Wonders Today* (London: Hodder & Stoughton, 1985), pp. 105–106.
4. Ibid., p. 103 (italics mine). It should be noted that in the 1992 edition of this book (see John Wimber with Kevin Springer, *Power Evangelism: Revised and Updated with Study Guide* (London: Hodder & Stoughton, 1992), p. 176) these words are modified to read ". . . he saw the connection between sickness and Satan."
5. Ibid., p. 102.
6. Ibid.
7. Wallace Benn and Mark Burkhill, *A Theological and Pastoral Critique of the Teachings of John Wimber,* Harold Wood Booklets, No. 1 (St. Peter's Church, Harold Wood, Romford, Essex, RM3 0QB, n.d.), p. 3.
8. Ibid.
9. *Power Evangelism,* p. 2.
10. David Lewis, *Healing: Fact or Fantasy?* (London: Hodder & Stoughton, 1989), pp. 262–263.
11. Philip Jensen with Kevin Springer, *Power Healing: Friend or Foe?, The Briefing,*

April 1990, pp. 7–8. It is possible that in this conversation Wimber was quoting numbers in a more impressionistic way than the authors assumed, but the point stands.

12. *Power Evangelism*, p. 101.
13. John Wimber with Kevin Springer, *Power Healing* (London: Hodder & Stoughton, 1986), p. 164.
14. Ibid., p. 32.
15. Ibid., p. 183.
16. Ibid., p. 154.
17. Ibid., p. 155.
18. Ibid., p. 16.
19. Ibid., p. 36.
20. e.g., Jensen and Payne, *John Wimber: Friend or Foe?*, p. 8.
21. *Power Healing*, pp. 166–167.
22. Jensen and Payne, *John Wimber: Friend or Foe?*, p. 9.
23. Ibid. The reports of John Wimber and his associates given in the booklet *John Wimber: Friend or Foe?* appear to me to require handling with a high degree of caution. Nevertheless, it does also appear to me that this particular report is likely to be an accurate one.
24. I took this line in a series of articles entitled, "Weighing up Wimber" in *Renewal* (January-March 1989).
25. J. I. Packer, "Signs and Wonders: Interview," *Touchstone*, January 1986, p. 7, cited in J. R. Coggins and Paul G. Hieberts (eds.), *Wonders and the Word* (Winnipeg: Kindred Press, 1989), p. 58.
26. Donald M. Lewis, "An Historian's Assessment," in Coggins and Hieberts, *Wonders and the Word*, p. 58.
27. Jürgen Moltmann, *The Way of Jesus Christ: Christology in Messianic Dimensions* (London: SCM Press, 1990), p. 110.
28. Gunstone, *Signs and Wonders*, p. 11.

Chapter 3

1. C. S. Lewis, *The Screwtape Letters* (London: Geoffrey Bles, 1942), p. 9.
2. See Chapter 2, note seven.
3. C. S. Lewis, *Broadcast Talks* (London: Geoffrey Bles, 1942), p. 46.
4. C. S. Lewis, *The Lion, the Witch, and the Wardrobe* (London: Geoffrey Bles, 1950).
5. Gustav Aulen, *Christus Victor*, trans. A. G. Herbert (London: SPCK, 1965).
6. J. M. Neale's translation, 1862.
7. Leon Festinger's now classic treatise *When Prophecy Fails* (University of Minnesota Press, 1956) is full of people with the paranoid delusions that only they can survive and flourish in a world ambushed by aliens and dangerous powers.
8. Dom Robert Petipierre (ed.), *Exorcism: The Findings of a Committee Converted by the Bishop of Exeter* (London: SPCK, 1972).
9. Jessie Penn-Lewis, *War on the Saints* (New York: Thomas Lowe, 1973).
10. Hagin's ministry, like Branham's, is replete with angelic ministrations.

Notes

11. Frank and Ida Mae Hammond, *Pigs in the Parlor* (Missouri: Impact Books, 1973).
12. See their *Christian, Set Yourself Free* (Chichester: New Wine Press, 1983).
13. Hammond, *Pigs in the Parlor*, p. 12.
14. Hear his tape "Spiritual Warfare" (Mobile, Alabama: Integrity Publications, 1983).
15. For a representative tape of Prince's earlier views, hear "Principalities and Powers" (Anchor Bay: Ministry Messages, undated); for an updated view of his belief in witchcraft, spells, and curses, see his *Blessing or Curse: You Can Choose!* (Milton Keynes: Word, 1990).
16. "Spiritual Warfare," op. cit. (n. 14).
17. Bill Subritzky, *Demons Defeated* (Chichester: Sovereign World Ltd.), p. 3.
18. Ibid., p. 8. On hearing this statement read out as part of a paper at a recent C. S. Lewis workshop at Sheffield, a "brother" from the Assemblies of God came up with an obvious solution to this demonic penetration: "Wear a condom!"—the eruptions of belly laughter from the 200 people at the conference would have cheered the heart of Luther and Lewis, both of whom believed that jeering and scornfulness, not respect or fearfulness, were the right attitudes toward the demonic.
19. Ibid., p. 69.
20. Ibid., p. 66.
21. Ibid., p. 149.
22. Hammond, *Pigs in the Parlor*, pp. 141–142.
23. Ibid, pp. 141–142.
24. The notion that the devil can be used by God as an instrument of His divine purposes is interestingly discussed in the correspondence between Don Calabria and C. S. Lewis. See *Letters, C. S. Lewis, Don Giovanni Calabria: A Study in Friendship*, trans. and ed. Martin Moynihan (London: Collins, 1989).
25. Wesley Carr, *Angels and Principalities* (Cambridge: Cambridge University Press, 1981); Walter Wink, *Naming the Powers: The Language of Power in the New Testament* (Philadelphia: Fortress Press, 1984; London: Marshall, Morgan & Scott, 1988). Wink's *Naming the Powers* is the first volume of a multi-volume work entitled *The Powers*.
26. Andrew Walker, *Enemy Territory: The Christian Struggle for the Modern World* (London: Hodder & Stoughton, 1987). American edition: Bristol Books, 1990.
27. Subritzky, *Demons Defeated*, p. 65.
28. Hammond, *Pigs in the Parlor*, p. 6.
29. Nigel Wright, *The Fair Face of Evil* (London: Marshall Pickering, 1989).
30. Subritzky, *Demons Defeated*, p. 35.
31. Frank Peretti, *This Presents Darkness* (Illinois: Crossway Books, 1986).
32. C.S. Lewis, *The Great Divorce* (London: Geoffrey Bles, 1945).

Chapter 4

1. From the point of view of systematic theology it could be said that theology has four tasks: (1) Eirenics (conciliation), (2) Polemics (controversial dis-

putation), (3) Apologetics (defense and promotion), (4) Dogmatics (interpretation and definition). Eirenical and polemical theology are for internal disputes within the Christian faith. Apologetics is the defense and promotion of Christianity to those outside the Church, while dogmatics is concerned with the explanation and clarification of orthodox doctrine. Eirenics and polemics are more typically reserved for theological issues of great importance, but not necessarily dogmatic ones. Nevertheless when dogmatic issues are at stake in the Church we can properly say that polemical theology (often of an astringent nature) is necessary.

2. We are grateful to Michael Beggs of Kings College London for suggesting to us the notion of the dogmatic core.

3. The fact, for example, that the Nicene Creed says of Jesus that "He was begotten not made" is precisely because Arius, a presbyter of the East, had claimed that Jesus as God's Son was only semi-divine—inferior to God because He was subsequent to or made by the Father.

4. J. MacArthur, Jr., *Charismatic Chaos* (Grand Rapids: Zondervan, 1992).

5. Though since the early days there have been movements of universalism, trinitarian modalism, and baptismal practices which have insisted on a "Jesus only" formula.

6. Reported in *Charisma,* August 1993, p. 24.

7. Osborn's teaching on faith as a force is very early and he may be more of an influence on the present-day Faith Movement than is realized.

8. In this respect Benny Hinn's most notorious (now recanted) doctrine that there were nine members of the Trinity seems to be based on ignorance and silliness, not mischievousness. It has to be hoped, as reported in *Christianity Today,* October 5, 1992, that Dr. J. Rodman Williams of Regent University can instill some basic Bible knowledge into Hinn.

9. Hendrickson, Mass. 1990. All quotations from this book are from the British edition (see note 18).

10. McConnell, op. cit., Chap. 3.

11. A. Walker, "We Believe," *Christianity Today,* Vol. 35, No. 5, April 29, 1991, pp. 25–27.

12. Quoted in McConnell, op. cit., p. 12.

13. Quoted in McConnell. ibid., p. 21.

14. The Word of Faith 13, 12, Dec. 1980, 14. This should not be read as Hagin saying that we can be like God being born into the world, because Hagin believes that Jesus was "born again" in hell. This being reborn spiritually—literally from fleshly limitation to spiritual power is available to all Christians. This is perhaps a classical example of how Faith teachers use traditional terms in unorthodox ways.

15. As visiting professor in evangelism at Southern Methodist University, it is part of Andrew Walker's brief to spend hours watching and analyzing televangelism. In Britain, too, his students try to follow the methodology of Copeland (the standard viewing being "Faith in the Future, Programs 1 & 2" H/W 23, 8, 91, Festival Copy V20988 625 PAL).

16. H. Hanegraaff, *Christianity in Crisis* (Oregon: Harvest House, 1993), p. 85.

17. C. Farah, *From the Pinnacle of the Temple* (Plainfield, N.J.: Logos, 1978), Gordon Fee, *The Disease of the Health & Wealth Gospels* (Beverly, Mass.:

Notes

Frontline Publishing, 1985), H. Hannegraaff, ibid., D. McConnell, op. cit.

18. Which is why The C. S. Lewis Centre published the book in Great Britain under the title *The Promise of Health and Wealth* (London: Hodder & Stoughton, 1990).

19. Op. cit., Part Three, Chapter 11.

20. McConnell makes much of the fact that some of Hagin's supernatural conversations are sometimes word for word pages from Kenyon's books. See McConnell, op. cit., Chapter 1.

21. Seattle, Kenyon's Gospel Publishing Society, 1945.

22. Quoted in Hanegraaff, op. cit., p. 383, note 45.

23. McConnell, op. cit., p. 120.

24. A popular, though curious, idea of Faith teaching is that the Jesus lifted up on the cross is satanic in nature because typologically the serpent raised up on the pole by Moses in the wilderness was a symbol of the devil.

25. Copeland in "Believer's Voice of Victory" program, April 21, 1990.

26. "The Price of It All," *Believer's Voice of Victory*, Sept. 19, 1991, quoted in Hanegraaff, op. cit., p. 383.

27. Quoted in McConnell, op. cit., p. 135.

28. We do need to be careful here. Strictly speaking it is wrong to assume that Jesus did not die a real death. Nor should we assume that the death of our Lord did not have a profound effect on the life of the divine Trinity. The Incarnation itself changes the eternal communion in the sense that from the conception of Jesus it is now and forever joined to creation. A sensitive yet bold way of handling these problems can be found in the writings of J. Moltmann. See his *The Crucified God* (London: SCM, 1974), and compare with *The Spirit of Life* (London: SCM, 1992).

29. This may very well be a weakness of much Pentecostal pneumatology.

30. Kenneth Copeland talks of such teaching as being "covered up and hidden in tradition." "What Happened From the Cross to the Throne" (Fort Worth: Kenneth Copeland Ministries, audio tape 2–0017, 1990). Discerning readers will have noticed that they have come across this title before!

31. From Nicea to Chalcedon the great Christological debates concerned the person of Christ.

32. See Gustav Aulen, *Christus Victor*, trans. A. G. Herbert (London: SPCK, 1965).

33. Indeed, Lewis self-consciously makes use of the ransom to the devil theory in the most famous of the Narnia chronicles. See Charles Taliaferro, "A Narnian Theory of the Atonement," *Scottish Journal of Theology* 41, 1988, pp. 75–92.

34. Sermon 261.1, quoted in Henery Bettenson (ed.), *The Latter Christian Fathers* (Oxford: Oxford University Press, 1977), p. 222.

35. Of the straightforward account of the chief priests and Pharisees who were afraid that Jesus would rise from the grave after three days as He had promised (Matthew 27:62–66).

36. *Institutes of the Christian Religion* 1, ed., J. T. McNeill (Philadelphia: Westminster Press, 1960), pp. 514–515.

37. Quoted in Hanegraaff, op. cit., p. 121.

38. "To Avoid a Modern Inquisition," *Ministries Today*, Sept./Oct. 1993. p. 8 ff.
39. See L. Carlyle May, "A Survey of Glossolalia and Related Phenomena in Non-Christian Religions" in *American Anthropologist*, 58, 1, 1956.
40. From Copeland's taped message, "Why All Are Not Healed," quoted in Hanegraaff, op. cit., p. 363.

Chapter 5

1. Jeremy Begbie, "The Spirituality of Renewal Music," *Anvil* 8.3 (1991), pp. 227–239.

Chapter 6

1. *Equipping the Saints* 3.4 (Fall 1989), pp. 4ff.
2. A full account of the Kansas City phenomenon is given in Michael Maudlin's, "Seers in the Heartland: Hot on the Trail of the Kansas City Prophets," *Christianity Today*, January 14, 1991, pp. 18–22.
3. *Equipping the Saints*, Special UK edition, Fall 1990, back cover.
4. John Wimber, "Revival Fire," *Renewal*, September 1991, p. 26.
5. Ibid., p. 27.
6. Cain speaks of this association in "Paul Cain Answers Some Tough Questions," *Equipping the Saints* 4.4 (Fall 1990), pp. 9ff.
7. Walter Hollenweger, *The Pentecostals* (London: SCM Press, 1972), pp. 354–357.
8. John Wimber, "A Response to Pastor Ernie Gruen's Controversy with Kansas City Fellowship," *Equipping the Saints*, Special UK edition, Fall 1990.

Chapter 7

1. Rudolf Bultmann, "New Testament and Mythology" in H.W. Bartsch (ed.) *Kerygma and Myth* (London: SPCK, 1953), p. 5.
2. A. Walker and J. S. Atherton, "An Easter Pentecostal Convention: The Successful Management of a "Time of Blessing," *The Sociological Review* 19.3 (August 1971).
3. Nigel Wright, *The Fair Face of Evil* (London: Marshall Pickering, 1989).

130253